About the Authors

Ken Boyle is from Dublin and his father's family was from the Ballinamore area of Leitrim. Ken worked in the financial sector in both Ireland and England. Since his retirement he has had the time to pursue a lifelong interest in recent Irish history. Ken's grandfather was Dr Muldoon's cousin. This is his first book.

Tim Desmond grew up in Cork city. He studied social science and journalism at UCC, before being taken on by RTÉ Radio after graduating. He has made a number of award-winning documentaries, which have taken him across Asia, Africa and Central America, with a particular focus on issues of social justice and the legacy of war. He now works full-time with the *Documentary On One* team at RTÉ Radio, producing his own documentaries and supervising the productions of independent documentary-makers.

THE MURDER OF

DR MULDOON

A SUSPECT PRIEST
A WIDOW'S FIGHT FOR JUSTICE

KEN BOYLE & TIM DESMOND

MERCIER PRESS

MERCIER PRESS
Cork
www.mercierpress.ie

© Ken Boyle and Tim Desmond, 2019

ISBN: 978 1 78117 690 0

A CIP record for this title is available from the British Library.

Printed and bound in the EU.

In memory of the victims of the
Irish Civil War 1922–23, and their families.

PROLOGUE

The gathering took place on a dark winter's evening on 17 January 1923, at the modest home of the parish priest in the small village of Cloone in County Leitrim. Three members of the local clergy were in attendance: the parish priest, Fr Deniston, a young curate named Edward Dunne, and Fr Edward Ryans, a curate from the neighbouring parish of Aughavas. The local doctor, Paddy Muldoon, and his wife, Rita, had driven the five miles or so from the town of Mohill for the meeting. But this wasn't a social gathering and any pleasantries exchanged soon gave way to the more serious matter at hand – the crisis pregnancy of Fr Ryans' housekeeper, Mary Kate Gallogly.

An hour or so into the meeting, Fr Ryans became highly agitated. Suddenly and without warning he pulled an automatic pistol from his cassock and began waving it around the room in a threatening manner. While everyone there was shocked by a man of the cloth using a lethal weapon to make his feelings known, only one person kept a written account of the events of that night: Rita Muldoon.[1]

In her own words: 'Fr. R produced Automatic and informed guests and especially Dr. M and myself that the weapon would account for 12 men, told us also that he carried this with impunity, that he had often escaped search when others were being held up and searched by Free S. Troops.'[2]

The priest was clearly angered by the intervention of Paddy and Rita Muldoon into his affairs, but while his behaviour that night was undoubtedly volatile and unhinged, it would only grow worse in the following weeks. His subsequent actions would create a scandal of national proportions, affecting a pregnant young woman, her child, and a peaceful, hard-working doctor and his family.

All of their lives would be changed forever.

CHAPTER 1

On the morning of 18 January 1923, Rita Lee Muldoon set off by train for Dublin.[1] She was making the journey as part of her duties to help look after the business of her husband Paddy's medical dispensary, a practice covering an area around the town of Mohill in south County Leitrim. Her trip started at Dromod station, the point at which the Midland Great Western railway service came closest to Mohill as it made its way from Sligo to Dublin.

The train journey to Dublin would have taken Rita through the towns of Longford and Mullingar, by now well established as centres of control by the nascent Irish Free State. In 1921 the Irish War of Independence had ended with a truce between the British and Irish sides. After difficult negotiations, a treaty was finalised that would bring about peace between Britain and Ireland. However, disagreement over the terms of this treaty within Ireland itself led to the reshaping of the conflict from a reasonably straightforward fight against the British to horrific domestic strife during 1922. The Civil War hampered the establishment of the Irish Free State, but by early 1923 the conflict had for the most part been reduced to acts of sabotage and revenge: roads and railways were targeted, locomotives and bridges demolished. Only weeks before Rita's journey to Dublin, stations in

Ballybunion, Listowel and Sligo were destroyed by the anti-Treaty forces.

As Rita sat looking out at the wintry landscape unfolding across the north midlands, she had time to reflect on the events of the previous evening. It was the first time she had become fully aware of Fr Edward Ryans' inherent violence and menace. Regardless of this, she was determined to pursue the priest in order to ensure that he did the right thing by his housekeeper, who was by now in the later stages of her pregnancy.

Rita's involvement with the local Mohill District Nursing Association, a voluntary group providing child welfare and midwifery services and other medical assistance to the poor, gave her an insight into the plight of young, and sometimes single, pregnant women in the area. When Mary Kate Gallogly's pregnancy came to her attention, probably through the nursing association, Rita became determined to ensure that the young woman be treated with the respect she deserved.[2] Even if that meant going up against the local priest.

***

Paddy and Rita Muldoon had been married almost five and a half years by January 1923. They had a young and growing family and were well settled in Mohill, a town familiar to Paddy because it lay about eight miles south of his family home.

Michael Patrick Muldoon, known as Paddy, was born on 3 September 1891, near the village of Fenagh in South Leitrim. The Muldoons were farmers and had lived in the townland of Cloodrumin for over half a century.[3] His father, Patrick Muldoon, was already a thirty-five-year-old widower when he married Paddy's mother, Mary Anne Duignan in January 1871 in the Catholic church at nearby Drumcong. Patrick Muldoon Senior had a modest farm but managed through hard work and good fortune to increase the holding to sixty acres when he acquired a plot from his brother, who emigrated to England around 1865.[4] By 1911 the Muldoon family were comfortable enough to have added a second floor to their house and to employ a young servant girl. The census of that year also reveals a sad reality of the times: Mary Anne Muldoon had given birth to fifteen children, but only nine still lived.

Paddy was the youngest of the family, born in 1891, and he benefited from that position. Three of his older brothers, James, Thomas and Joseph, and a sister, Roseanne, had emigrated to the west coast of America between 1898 and 1910. They regularly sent money home to their parents, remittances which most likely financed the enlarging of the family home and helped provide a good education for Paddy. He attended St Mary's College, the Marist secondary school in Dundalk. From there he went on to study medicine at the National University of Ireland in Dublin.[5] Paddy attended university during the significant period of the 1916 Rising and its aftermath, and it was during these tumultuous times that he met and fell in love with Rita Lee.

Margaret, known as Rita, was four years younger than Paddy. Although they both came from relatively prosperous backgrounds in rural Ireland, Rita's family were firmly in the middle class. The Lees, who sometimes went by the grander-sounding surname of Hession-Lee, were a Catholic family that had made significant progress up the social ladder. Rita's father, Bernard Lee, was originally from Roundstone in County Galway but had moved to nearby Clifden, attracted by the better opportunities there. He married Margaret Hession and they had a family of four girls and four boys. Bernard was a successful merchant and publican who ran his business from the premises in Market Street that is now occupied by Vaughan's pub and bistro. His daughters went to good schools and Rita's older sisters, May and Delia, had the privilege of attending finishing schools in France. Rita and her younger sister, Imelda, were sent to the Dominican nuns in Eccles Street, Dublin. Two of her brothers, Michael and Alfred, qualified as doctors, while Bernard Ambrose, or Amby as he was known, became a solicitor.[6]

Unusually for women in Ireland at that time, Rita Lee had continued her education to university level, studying medicine in Dublin. A strikingly attractive woman, she was not particularly tall, but had a heart-shaped face and high cheekbones. In photographs from the early 1920s she has a strong, direct gaze. The family was undoubtedly proud of

Rita's academic achievements, which is why it must have dismayed them when she decided, quite suddenly, to abandon her medical studies to get married.[7]

On 14 August 1917, just two days before his registration as a doctor, Paddy Muldoon married Margaret Lee at the Catholic church in Clifden, County Galway. She was just twenty-one years old; he was twenty-five. Rita was already expecting their first child when they married.

The recently qualified doctor and his new wife left Ireland almost immediately, a decision likely influenced by a desire to put some distance between themselves and their families, who were not happy about the circumstances of the marriage. Paddy and Rita moved to Wales so that Paddy could take up a position assisting a general practitioner, Dr Howell Evans, who described his practice as 'a large panel and colliery practice in Monmouthshire where exceptional opportunities daily occur of gaining experience in Surgery, Midwifery, and General Practice'.[8] Paddy and Rita's first child, Patrick Bernard Llewellyn, known as Llew, was

Paddy and Rita Muldoon with their two oldest children, Llew and Olwyn, in 1920. (© The Muldoon/Donnelly family.)

born in Monmouthshire on 30 January 1918, just five-and-a-half months after they were married.[9]

Despite the reasons for their move to Wales, it appears that shortly after the birth of Llew the Muldoons desired to return to their home country. Neither, it seemed, wanted to raise a child in exile. They had been in Wales for just six months when the young doctor applied to move back to Ireland, to his home county of Leitrim, where a large public medical practice, known as the Rynn Dispensary District of Mohill, about eight miles from where Paddy had grown up, had become vacant in March 1918.

His application met with some resistance, however. The Local Government Board in Dublin didn't want the vacancy filled at the time, particularly by a young doctor whose expertise could be utilised on the Western Front. The board's main priority was providing doctors for the Royal Army Medical Corps, as Britain remained engaged in the Great War. This meant that there was effectively a ban on recruitment. However, the Mohill Board of Guardians, reflecting the growing nationalist and anti-conscription fervour at the time, disregarded the Local Government Board's request that the position not be filled and set about appointing Paddy Muldoon. This resulted in the Local Government Board relenting and agreeing to confirm his position, initially on a temporary basis.[10]

Rita and Paddy Muldoon arrived back in Ireland with their young child at a time when the world was facing one of the greatest medical challenges of the twentieth century: the Spanish flu pandemic.[11] The flu was sweeping through the community of South Leitrim just as Paddy was taking over the practice. The run-up to the general election of December 1918, which saw Sinn Féin emerge as the dominant political force in Ireland, helped spread the outbreak of the flu, with its mass meetings and countrywide movement of party activists. In such an unprecedented medical emergency, the Rynn Dispensary area, sixteen miles long and six miles broad, was lucky to have the services of a young, energetic doctor.[12]

A local newspaper reported on the challenges facing the young Muldoon: 'He was on his feet night and day attending his patients. No distance or circumstances hindered him in the discharge of his onerous duties and his name was popular in every household in South Leitrim.'[13] By the time the Spanish flu pandemic had worked its way through the world's population, which included more than 20,000 victims in Ireland, Paddy Muldoon had earned the respect of the people he served.

As a result, by 1923 he and Rita were firmly established and respected in South Leitrim. Now thirty-one, Paddy had become used to long hours and a challenging workload. In spite of these, photographs of him at the time show a round, amiable face, which gave him the appearance of a much younger man. Known for his fine physique and good horse-riding skills, he was obliging in his work and personal life, and clearly loved his role as a country doctor. He was a regular sight rushing to patients spread across a wide area in his Model T Ford touring car, a rare enough sight on the back roads of the county at the time. On occasion he cut a particular dash travelling on his motorbike, a Douglas 250cc tourer, capable of forty-five miles an hour on the winding country roads.

Rita was just as busy as her husband. As well as looking after the three young children they had at this stage – Llew, Olwyn and Des – and running a busy household, Rita managed the accounts of the medical practice. Her journey to Dublin on 18 January was for the purpose of meeting the Paymaster General of the Free State army in relation to payments for her husband's services to troops. In addition to his main occupation as a dispensary doctor, Paddy Muldoon also had a role as a medical officer to the National Army.[14]

The Muldoons had, by then, been involved in providing medical care in South Leitrim during four years of conflict, starting with the War of Independence and continuing into the Civil War that followed. Paddy provided medical care to both sides in the Civil War without fear or favour and would often have someone from the government side coming in the front door of the house to attend his surgery at the same time as an anti-Treaty supporter was leaving by the back. Still, Rita had taken the precaution of sewing a large red cross on Paddy's overcoat, so that when he was out on calls in the countryside he wouldn't be mistaken for a combatant by either side.[15]

However, it wasn't the general conflict that was on Rita's mind that January day, but the potential for more trouble from the priest who had produced a weapon the previous night. She would later come to learn that the entire town of Mohill, it seemed, was aware of the out-of-control behaviour of this priest, and his later activities would come as no surprise to many locals. It was common knowledge, after all, that Ryans was deeply involved with anti-Treaty forces in the area, a group who were causing no end of trouble.

Her railway journey to Dublin ended safely at the Broadstone depot, less than a mile north of the city centre. As she left the station, Rita, who was pregnant again, could not have known how significant this railway terminus would become in the weeks ahead, with a pivotal and bizarre event in the Muldoons' and Ryans' story playing out in its vicinity.

CHAPTER 2

Coolebawn House, the Muldoon family home and surgery, was a substantial five-bedroom, semi-detached property located on Station Road on the southeast side of the town of Mohill. The road, which took its name from the narrow-gauge railway station that had opened in 1887, used to run parallel to the railway line before curving to the left over a small, partially culverted tributary of the River Rinn, turning into Main Street and rising in a gradual climb to the imposing Catholic church of Saint Patrick on the western edge of Mohill.[1]

Mohill sits neatly at the southern end of County Leitrim, an area pockmarked by small lakes sitting among some reasonably good farmland. The name itself comes from the Irish word for soft or spongy ground, although it is far enough south of the large upland bogs of the Arigna hills. The town's history stretches back 1,500 years to a monastery founded by Saint Manachán.[2] Over the centuries the area was subjected to invasion and plantation, and the monastery was closed during the reign of King Henry VIII. In the seventeenth century the town and some of the adjacent lands passed into the ownership of the Crofton family. The Clements family, who owned land outside the town, included William Sydney Clements, the 3rd Earl of Leitrim, who is remembered as one of the most notorious landlords of nineteenth-century Ireland.

By the 1920s Mohill had established itself as a moderately prosperous market town with twenty-nine public houses and a hinterland population of about 2,000. The Muldoons were happy here, despite the troubles with the ongoing Civil War.

As they were having such a busy and successful time in Mohill, Paddy and Rita needed help with their growing family. They found it in a young woman named Kate Kerr. Like Ryans' housekeeper, Mary Kate Gallogly, nineteen-year-old Kate Kerr was from the local area. The young woman became close to the Muldoon children and loved her life with them, happy to take care of them while Rita and Paddy built their life in Mohill. The children were very fond of Kate, and Paddy and Rita intended to help her get a recognised qualification as a nanny when the time came for her to move on.[3]

For all of Rita's busyness, however, when she returned to Mohill from Dublin that January of 1923, she had made her mind up about one thing. She would keep a close eye on Fr Ryans and his activities.

***

Edward Ryans was curate in the parish of Aughavas, about eight miles northeast of the town of Mohill and just a few dozen miles from his family home. The Ryans family were coal miners, originally working the pits around Durham, in the northeast of England, for a couple of generations before Edward's father, Joseph, brought his family back to Ireland when he came to work in the Arigna coal mines in County Roscommon in the early 1890s. Joseph Ryans became a mine engineer and the family, eventually, were able to move to the large, well-appointed Knockranny House in the village of Keadue in Roscommon, a few miles from the Leitrim border.

Born in Durham in 1886, Edward Ryans came to live in Ireland as a young child in the 1890s with the rest of his family. His father's position as an engineer in the successful Arigna coal mines provided the money for the young Edward to attend St Mel's secondary school in Longford town as a boarder. He was a talented student and took a path familiar to many Irish Catholic families at that time. He was the second eldest and, as with many in this position (the eldest usually took over the family farm, although in this case the Ryans weren't farmers), he was destined for a life in the priesthood.

In 1904 Ryans progressed from St Mel's to Maynooth in County Kildare to study for the priesthood. As a student of theology, Ryans excelled at Saint Patrick's seminary in Maynooth, where some of the brightest talents studied hard and prepared for religious life. He was exceptional at French, winning prizes for French grammar and essays in the language on 'Gothic Architecture'.[4] In June 1911, on taking his vows at ordination, the twenty-five-year-old novice became Fr Edward Ryans.[5]

Fr Ryans was no ordinary priest. His first appointment was as curate to the parish of Annaduff in Leitrim, but it was after he moved to Rathcline parish in neighbouring County Longford in 1913 that his political reputation began to develop.[6] By 1917 he had become heavily involved in the growing republican movement and by the end of the year he had been elected president of the Executive of Sinn Féin Clubs in South Longford.[7]

In the spring of 1917 republicans from all over Ireland descended on South Longford to campaign for what would be a famous victory for Joseph McGuinness, the Sinn Féin electoral candidate. Sinn Féin was initially founded as a nationalist party that advocated change by non-violent means, but it had been associated with radical political activity in Ireland and, incorrectly, with the Easter Rising, by the British and the main nationalist party, the Irish Parliamentary Party (IPP), which favoured Home Rule. After the Rising, Sinn Féin benefited from growing nationalist anger and resentment over the execution of the Rising's leaders and the imprisonment of large numbers of people, many of whom had taken no active part in the rebellion. This by-election would be one of the party's first attempts to gain political legitimacy.[8]

Fr Ryans found himself in the right place to play a central role in the campaign to elect Joseph McGuinness, an Irish Volunteer who was actually in prison in England at the time of the election for his part in the Rising. The campaign gave rise to the slogan 'Put him in to get him out'.[9]

One campaigning republican sympathiser was Elizabeth Corr, a member of Cumann na mBan, who had travelled from Belfast.[10] Her account of the election campaign reveals that 'the majority of the parish priests, headed by the Bishop were against us.' However, she goes on to describe meeting 'the famous Fr Ryans who is looked upon as a second Fr O'Flanagan', a reference to another rebel cleric who would later become the joint national vice-president of Sinn Féin.[11]

Fr Ryans told Elizabeth and her campaigning group that 'in his village, Lanesboro [*sic*], McGuinness polled nine-tenths of the vote'. This left her with the belief that 'if we had a Father O'Flanagan or a Father Ryans in every parish in Ireland Sinn Féin would sweep the country'.[12] McGuinness ultimately won the by-election for Sinn Féin by the tightest of margins, a mere thirty-seven votes.

While Ryans' success in gaining votes for Sinn Féin among his parishioners might have captivated Miss Corr, it made a poor impression on his bishop. After all, Bishop Hoare and the rest of the Catholic hierarchy had long given their strong support to John Redmond's IPP.[13] Many years later Ryans would record that his difficult relationship with Bishop Hoare, his diocesan superior, began around the time of the South Longford by-election of May 1917.[14]

Sure enough, shortly after the election, in September 1917, Fr Ryans was moved to the parish of Abbeylara in North Longford. It is highly likely that this move was a direct result of the bishop's displeasure with the curate's involvement in the by-election. By chance, however, this move brought Ryans further into republican circles. Abbeylara is not far from Ballinalee, the home place of Seán Mac Eoin, the legendary Longford IRA leader. Ryans and Mac Eoin became friends around this time because of their shared republican feelings and activities.

By the time he arrived in Aughavas parish in South Leitrim in 1918,

Commandant Seán Mac Eoin at Athlone Barracks, 1922. (Courtesy of Mercier Archive)

Edward Ryans' reputation was based more on his political activities than his clerical duties or previous academic achievements. He had become something of a hero within the republican movement, a reputation that had left him at serious odds with his religious superiors.

Once in Aughavas, Ryans continued to combine his clerical duties with political activity. He even served as a judge in the republican Sinn Féin courts, a system of arbitration set up to replace the crown courts and help undermine British rule by replacing a crucial part of the existing British State's machinery in Ireland.[15] This was another in a series of roles and activities that put Ryans at odds with the Church around this time. His political activities are probably why, although he had served as a priest for almost a decade and had been an acclaimed scholar at Maynooth, Ryans never attained the prestigious position of parish priest.

However, it was not just these activities that got Ryans in trouble. While in Aughavas he shared clerical duties with a Fr Joseph McGivney. One of the disputes Ryans had with the local church at this time involved arguments with McGivney over money, to the point that McGivney announced from the pulpit that Ryans wasn't to be entrusted with any parish dues or revenues, evidently because they weren't being properly accounted for.[16]

The heroic reputation that Ryans had cultivated within the republican movement also threatened to lose its shine for a time, when he became involved in another controversy about money. In his role as a judge in the Sinn Féin courts, Ryans had a responsibility for handling fines imposed by the court and passing on the funds collected, as well as other monies received in his capacity as a member of the local Sinn Féin Executive. This money was ultimately destined for the financing of the War of Independence. However, a colleague of Ryans in Leitrim Sinn Féin, Michael Reilly of Aughavas, became annoyed about a number of issues involving Ryans and wrote a formal letter of complaint about the priest. It seems Ryans had not provided a receipt for £53 collected in October 1919 for the Self Determination Fund administered centrally by Michael Collins. When Ryans was challenged on this issue, he apparently claimed that 'he gave the money to Michael Collins personally and that he neither asked for or got a receipt from him'.[17]

Ryans' difficulties with parish and Sinn Féin finances suggest that he may have been misappropriating funds to supplement his meagre income as a rural cleric.

Ryans was also unusual for a priest at that time, and especially a rural curate, in that he owned a car. A Liberty Six cost about £500 at the time, much more than a year's salary for most people. Ryans would later claim that he purchased his Liberty Six, which had many extras, for that price.[18] It would seem that he purchased the car from a Fr Thomas Tubman, a Ballinamore native, who had been on an extended holiday from Reno, Nevada, where he served as parish priest.[19] The car would have been exchanged before Tubman's return to New York on 24 November 1920, the very same month that Fr Ryans' disagreement over parish finances with his parish priest, Fr McGivney, came to a head.[20]

Given the questions raised about his handling of both parish and Sinn Féin funds, and his unearthing of a large amount of money to buy the car, it certainly seems that Ryans had found his own way of financing a more expensive lifestyle than that of a typical rural cleric.

Despite these issues, the rebel priest was able to deepen his involvement in politics and, to an extent, in military activity during the War of Independence. His brother Vincent and sister Margaret were very active in the IRA and Cumann na mBan respectively in the Arigna area, and Edward Ryans himself became a subject of interest to the crown forces on numerous occasions. It is clear that his involvement certainly went beyond his role as a politically outspoken priest and it becomes evident from his letters at this time that, because of his more militant activities, Fr Ryans did not feel safe living in the parish house at Aughavas. Consequently, he spent periods of time on the run.

Life as a fugitive, even a part-time one, compromised Ryans' ability to carry out his clerical duties and put further pressure on his bishop to deal effectively with this rebel cleric. His strong commitment to the republican cause remained, however, in spite of the bishop's disapproval of his involvement in political affairs.[21]

The precarious situation that Ryans was in with his superiors dragged on until 22 June 1921, when the partition of Ireland by the British government was formally inaugurated with the opening of the Northern Ireland parliament in Belfast. Peace negotiations between the British government and Sinn Féin, which had been progressing intermittently since late the previous year, were given fresh impetus.

On 11 July 1921 the Truce to end the War of Independence came into effect. The arrival of peace brought great relief, with the lifting of the general sense of fear and despondency that had permeated the country for almost two-and-a-half years. Men like Edward Ryans, who had been on the run, suddenly reappeared and were feted as heroes in their localities. This relief was not to last, however.

The Treaty that followed negotiations during the Truce was ratified in Dáil Éireann by a narrow majority in early January 1922, after weeks of bitter argument and dissent among the hitherto united Sinn Féin. Despite the ratification, the country was clearly divided about the Treaty.

On 22 January, Fr Ryans presided over a meeting of the South Leitrim Executive of Sinn Féin Clubs, held in Mohill, to discuss the Treaty. The Executive voted overwhelmingly to approve the Treaty and nominated Fr Ryans to represent them at the Sinn Féin Ard Fheis to be held in Dublin the following month.[22]

It seems that Ryans was initially a firm supporter of the Treaty. He is described in a newspaper report as speaking strongly in its favour, along with a number of local members of the Dáil, at a meeting in Carrick-on-Shannon on St Patrick's Day 1922.[23] This meeting was held to launch the pro-Treaty electoral campaign for the general election of June 1922, which would allow the public their say on the Treaty.

The outcome of the June election was clear-cut, with over seventy per cent of the successful candidates representing parties who supported acceptance of the Treaty. Despite this emphatic demonstration of the people's will, however, the dissenters would not accept the majority's decision to take the path of gradual procurement of a republic. Early in the morning of 28 June 1922, with a certain inevitability, the

Civil War commenced when the National Army attacked the anti-Treaty forces who had barricaded themselves inside Dublin's Four Courts complex.[24]

Perhaps because of family pressure, Ryans switched allegiance to the anti-Treaty side in the Civil War, putting himself firmly on the side of those fighting against the newly formed Irish Free State. For the remainder of 1922 it became clear that he'd picked the losing side, as the anti-Treaty forces were put on the back foot, eventually being driven away from the populated areas and gradually losing numbers.

However, one beneficial consequence of Leitrim's remote location near the newly established border with Northern Ireland – at least from the anti-Treaty side's perspective – was that many combatants from the North moved south, and a large column of fighters gathered and remained at large in the Arigna area on the Roscommon/Leitrim border.

Despite his switch of allegiance, Ryans had connections and loyalties on both sides in the war. Many of those on the pro-Treaty side were friends and colleagues from before the split and this was used by Ryans to his advantage. When he boasted to the Muldoons at the Cloone meeting that he could act with impunity, he had good reason to make that claim, given his reputation and connections. After all, the overall responsibility for security on behalf of the Free State in the area fell on Major General Seán Mac Eoin, the former Sinn Féin colleague and friend of Ryans from his days in Longford.

As the Civil War continued into 1923, the increasingly beleaguered anti-Treaty side resorted to more desperate tactics, and the area of South Leitrim in particular had a certain air of lawlessness. Fr Edward Ryans was at this time a familiar sight in South Leitrim, driving his Liberty Six motor car around the locality.

Ryans' parish was in the area covered by the medical practice of Paddy Muldoon. On his rounds to treat patients, the young doctor would often drive his five-seater Ford Model T past the church where Ryans said Mass and carried out his other clerical duties. This being small-town Ireland, everybody knew everybody else, especially those in positions of power and responsibility. The two men moved in the same social circles and had developed something of a friendship based in part on their mutual acquaintances. That relationship changed dramatically during 1922, however, when one of Paddy Muldoon's patients became pregnant: eighteen-year-old Mary Kate Gallogly, the priest's housekeeper.

Muldoon family records show that Paddy and Rita Muldoon became aware of the pregnancy long before Ryans drew his gun at that meeting in January 1923.[25] The couple had persuaded – or more likely pressured – Ryans to do the right thing and stand by Mary Kate. That would explain why she wasn't sent, like most pregnant single women at the time, to a Magdalene home. Instead, towards the end of 1922, she had been sent to lodgings in Dublin to await the birth of her child.

Any chance Ryans had of salvaging his reputation and position as a Catholic priest in the longer term was put severely at risk by this pregnancy and everything that it implied. The political reputation he cultivated over the years would also be destroyed by what would be considered a scandal. Ryans was clearly aware of this, as he mentions later in a statement that he sought to 'keep it cloaked'.[26] He clearly believed that news of the pregnancy could potentially end his career as both a cleric and a political activist.

One thing is for sure: Rita Muldoon's close monitoring of Fr Ryans around this time – taking note of incidents he was involved in and asking people she knew to report to her what they heard of his activities – posed a very real threat to Ryans because, along with Paddy, she had knowledge of the circumstances of the housekeeper's pregnancy.

CHAPTER 3

Mary Kate Gallogly was just a teenager when she was taken on to work as housekeeper for Fr Edward Ryans. Born in 1903, she grew up on a small farm a few miles from the village of Aughavas. Her parents had married late and both were in their thirties by the time Mary Kate arrived. She had one sibling, an older brother, and the family lived with Mary Kate's grandfather, Peter, on a smallholding in the townland of Drumshanbo North in the Aughavas area. They resided in a thatched, mud-walled, three-roomed cottage, with a cow house, a piggery and a small barn.[1]

A young woman like Mary Kate had few opportunities for anything apart from farm work, emigration or an early marriage. The prospect of being taken on as a priest's house-keeper would have been exciting for a teenager, given the re-sponsibility and prestige of such a posting.

There is no known record of any written testimony by Mary Kate as to the circumstances of her pregnancy and the events that changed her life in 1923. While others involved took the opportunity to talk and write about what followed, she appears to have remained silent. According to Ryans, Mary Kate had 'acted as housekeeper in my house for a number of weeks in place of her cousin who had unexpectedly got married'.[2]

Edward Ryans took the highly unusual step of sending Mary Kate to Dublin in the later months of her pregnancy, paying for her accommodation himself and giving her clear instructions as to how she was to present herself in Dublin when the time came for the birth of the baby. She had probably never been to a city of the size and sophistication of Dublin, and we don't know who, if anyone, visited her. She was still just a teenager when she arrived there, sometime in November 1922, alone in a strange city. Ryans clearly had the young woman under his complete control. She told none of her friends about the pregnancy; it was a secret she must have been instructed to keep.

For most single women who found themselves pregnant in 1920s Ireland, life was very difficult. Mary Kate's pregnancy outside marriage was one of about 1,700 reported in Ireland each year during the 1920s (although there was an acknowledgement that unreported pregnancies and births could have doubled this number at least). It was a figure that would rise as the years went on, in spite of the best efforts of the new Free State with the support of the Church to reduce the number.[3]

The female body, and the role of women as mothers in particular, was to become a central focus of concern to the State and the Irish Catholic Church for decades to come. In the 1920s there was a political and religious narrative suggesting that the rate of illegitimate births had been the result of the stationing of British troops in Ireland; that the servicing of garrisons under British rule had led to many women falling from grace and now it was time to 'return the nation to purity'. There were plenty of references to the 'collapse of chastity' in pamphlets from lectures by members of the clergy.[4] The notion of a priest's housekeeper becoming pregnant would have been anathema to the story of a Church restoring the nation to purity.

In Mary Kate's case, she was fortunate only in that she wasn't sent to one of the 'special institutions' increasingly used around this time. Mother and baby homes run by the religious orders were often the only option for women without means who were in this situation. Instead, she was sent in a private capacity to give birth at Holles Street maternity hospital. She registered herself under a false name, Kate Brown, on arrival at the hospital, where she gave birth to her daughter on Monday 29 January 1923.

On her daughter's arrival, Mary Kate named her Rose. Rose Brown. She gave no name for the father of her child and gave her address simply as 'Bushwood' in Roscommon (the county where Ryans' family home was located).[5] No place called Bushwood existed then or now.

We can imagine Mary Kate, exhausted and alone, in Holles Street hospital, looking out on the broad Georgian streets of Dublin, at the northeast corner of Merrion Square. On the opposite side of the square to the hospital were Government Buildings. In early 1923 the buildings were the locus of the emerging Free State government, which was just months in existence by then.

As the young mother held her newborn baby to her chest, she would have looked across at the physical centre of power, likely praying that everything would work out for her and her child.

***

As Mary Kate Gallogly lay in the maternity hospital in Dublin with her baby, back in Leitrim, during the early days of February 1923, Edward Ryans was acting less like a priest and more like a man losing control.

The Civil War was entering its final phase and the National Army had the task of clearing out the remaining anti-Treaty fighters, or 'Irregulars' as they were disparagingly called by their opponents. Attacks at this point were being carried out only intermittently and the war was just months away from coming to a complete end. There were fewer and fewer areas of the country controlled to any degree by those opposed to the Treaty, but in places like South Leitrim the level of Free State control remained constantly under threat.[6]

The Catholic Church had declared itself firmly pro-Treaty in its October 1922 pastoral to the faithful, and had begun to denounce the anti-Treaty campaign and refuse the sacraments to fighters. However, in spite of direct pressure from his bishop, Joseph Hoare, and the general view of his Church, Fr Ryans continued to side with – and by all accounts fight alongside – his fellow anti-Treaty rebels.

One of the strongholds of the anti-Treaty side was the

area in which the Ryans family lived. Up to seventy fighters were holed up in the mountainous area around Arigna to the northwest of Mohill. The area was about twenty-five miles northwest of the parish in which Ryans served. The Arigna flying column of anti-Treaty fighters was led by men like Ned Bofin and the Cull brothers. Edward Ryans' brother Vincent also played a key leadership role. Utilising local support, the group operated with relative ease, raiding Civic Guard stations and National Army barracks, and attempting to dismantle railways and other infrastructure.

One incident involving Fr Ryans took place in Leitrim just three days after Rose Brown was born. This was an attack on the town of Ballinamore on 1 February. Ballinamore lies about fifteen miles north of Mohill and is similar in size. In a daring raid, a combined anti-Treaty force of about 150 men overran the town, capturing and destroying the National Army barracks and damaging the town's railway infrastructure.[7] The barracks was taken after a short firefight and then blown up. The train station was destroyed and, as well as losing their arms and transport tenders, thirty-five Free State National Army soldiers were rounded up and taken back to Arigna and then into the mountains as prisoners when the anti-Treaty force withdrew from the town.[8]

There is little doubt that Ryans took part in this raid. The large attacking force would have required considerable transport and Ryans, with his Liberty Six, was in the perfect position to provide assistance. He is believed to have used his car to transport fighters and equipment during the raid and was reported to have been disarmed at one point by Free State army officers in Ballinamore before they themselves were overcome by anti-Treaty forces.[9]

Vincent Ryans was a full-time member of the Arigna column responsible for the attack on Ballinamore with the assistance of their comrades from the South Leitrim area. Another of the anti-Treaty fighters involved in the raid on Ballinamore that day would play a crucial role in the service of Fr Edward Ryans in the coming weeks.[10]

Born in 1899, John Charles Keegan was from a farming background and lived with his mother and siblings near

John Charles Keegan (left) with Éamon de Valera, Austin Stack
and a National Army officer in Arbour Hill Prison in 1924.
(Courtesy of Mercier Archive)

Cattan, a few miles from the town of Mohill. He had taken part in the War of Independence, originally as a dispatcher, and later in charge of communications for his local Cloone unit of the IRA. There is some evidence, in the form of a letter sent by Keegan in 1974 to Erskine Childers, that he suffered a severe pistol-whipping at the hands of the RIC during this time. Like Ryans, Keegan initially took the pro-Treaty side in the Civil War, even becoming a member of the National Army, before dramatically changing sides.[11]

Keegan was injured during the Ballinamore attack and treated for his wounds afterwards by a member of Cumann na mBan, Bridget Doherty, from Cloone near Aughavas, one of the women who formed part of the support network for the fighters in the area. In an account of her involvement in the War of Independence and the Civil War that she wrote a number of years later, she gives an insight into how the social norms of the rural world were put aside in order to serve the cause of those involved in the fighting: 'I carried dispatches for Seán O'Farrell Bgd [Brigade] O/C. I nursed him on too [sic] occasions when he had a bad cold. I gave him my bed and also did guard for him and, I kept his revolver and ammunition and correspondence during his sick period.'[12]

Bridget Doherty's account also mentions that the Cloone Company of Cumann na mBan received their training in first aid from Dr Paddy Muldoon. She goes on to mention cooking for the anti-Treaty fighters in November 1922, including one 'J C Keegan', and that, after the Ballinamore raid, 'I nursed J C Keegan, wounded by Free State soldiers at Cloone'.[13]

The anti-Treaty gang operating in the Cloone–Aughavas area was a tight-knit group. And soon further nefarious activity by Ryans and Keegan would tie the two anti-Treaty supporters even more closely together.

***

A few days after the Ballinamore raid, Rita Muldoon made the short journey from her home in Coolebawn House to the National Army barracks in Mohill. She was trying to confirm reports she had from other sources about Ryans' anti-Treaty activities in the area. However, in this case she had no luck. In her written account of the time there is an entry from Monday 5 February:

> About this time, got information about charges against Fr. R eg. ------? in Fenagh, Mohill, Ballinamore. Made enquiries in Mohill barracks about doings in Ballinamore and failed to get any information from Military.[14]

Rita was more fortunate the following day, when she visited the National Army area headquarters in nearby Longford town. During this particular visit to Longford, she questioned some officers about Fr Ryans' involvement in the attack on Ballinamore. She spoke with officers who had been present both before and during the attack, and managed to get information from some of them in confidence. She was given the names of officers who had witnessed Fr Ryans' actions during the raid. They told her that they had managed to disarm him before their barracks was eventually captured and the National Army was forced to surrender.[15]

Information like this would have normally led to the arrest of Ryans, possession of weapons being a serious offence. Yet Ryans somehow continued to act with impunity.

Rita wrote to the two officers who were directly involved in the disarming of Ryans at their current locations in Athlone and the Curragh. On 6 February she writes:

> In Longford, saw some Military officers present in Ballinamore previous to the capture of barracks and during attack and got some facts stated, but under confidence. Had letter to officer in Athlone and Curragh who had disarmed Fr R and witnessed his actions there, never received any answer to these letters.[16]

There is no doubt that Rita was actively trying to get the authorities to do something about the priest during these weeks. Furthermore, she did have contacts and relationships with senior military figures in the Free State army. For instance, the Muldoons had received a Christmas card only weeks before from the military commander in the area, Major General Seán Mac Eoin, and his wife. Clearly Rita wanted this volatile and potentially dangerous person dealt with before he had a chance to do something serious to her family.

The army, however, had bigger issues to worry about. On the very same day that Rita questioned the National Army officers in Longford about the attack on Ballinamore, the Arigna column carried out a particularly ruthless raid on the nearby town of Ballyconnell, which resulted in two civilian deaths. That same week in February, Richard Mulcahy, the minister for defence, said of the raid:

> … there is this particular type of madness amongst a section of the people in the country who are armed, who are supported in their madness by feeling that they are following an ideal and by gathering to themselves all the phrases and all the words that have supported our national struggle in the past …[17]

Later, in the same Dáil debate, Mulcahy spoke about the state of the security situation in the South Leitrim area:

> Anybody who knows the hinterland of mountains lying behind Ballinamore and Ballyconnell will understand that for the work we have to do in that area we have not sufficient troops effectively to control those mountains and to get that band of Irregulars that we know have been hiding there for some time.[18]

He also bemoaned the lenience of the existing Free State garrisons:

… some of our men in that area, not undertaking to believe that those men were as black as their present deeds have painted them, have, contrary to orders and contrary to the spirit of discipline in the Army, been carrying on a sort of negotiation with them [the anti-Treaty forces] …[19]

There was a quick follow-up to the minister's concerns about the progress of the war in the area, however, when a major offensive was launched. Over 300 Free State soldiers with Lewis machine guns, motorised transport and an armoured car were sent to search the mountains near Arigna to root out the column and to enforce the authority of the Free State in the surrounding area. Edward Ryans was likely stuck somewhere in the middle of it, helping the anti-Treaty forces in whatever way he could.

At the same time, Mary Kate Gallogly was experiencing the first days of motherhood in Dublin. She may well have imagined that she and baby Rose would stay together and that their future would hold some promise. She had kept her word to the priest to tell nobody she encountered at the hospital the reality of her situation, or of Ryans' involvement in her pregnancy. Perhaps Mary Kate stayed loyal to Ryans in the hope of a good outcome for herself and her child, and trusting a promise from Ryans that he would look after things for her and the baby.

What happened next, however, would change all that.

CHAPTER 4

Edward Ryans arrived in Dublin to collect Mary Kate and baby Rose on 13 February. Later that day, shortly after seven o'clock in the evening, a group of three women were gathered at the front doors of neighbouring tenement buildings on Lower Dominick Street in the north inner city, when something caught their attention.

Today, the remaining Georgian houses in that area of Dublin are part of the internationally recognised architectural heritage of the city, elegant and high-ceilinged, with ornate plasterwork, wide sweeping staircases and long sash windows. In 1923, however, many of the houses were run-down, multiple-occupancy dwellings, or tenements, on streets long abandoned by the original well-off occupiers. The women and families who lived along the street, and particularly at numbers 15 and 16, were among the poorest class in Dublin at that time.[1]

One of the three women, Catherine Ball, was first to notice the young couple with the baby. She was standing at the door of number 15, the tenement building in which she and her family lived. The couple passed along, coming from the direction of Saint Saviour's church and Dominican priory, about a hundred yards away.[2] It was a wet evening and had been raining in Dublin for most of the day. Catherine could see that the young woman was carrying a baby in her arms. They walked on a little further before turning left into Granby Lane, a narrow side street that led east.

Catherine noticed that something was not right. The woman appeared distressed. She called to her neighbours, Christina O'Brien and Mary Dalton, who were standing in the doorway of number 16. The three women decided to follow the couple around the corner into Granby Lane.

The 'couple' were, of course, Fr Edward Ryans and Mary Kate Gallogly. The pair abruptly turned back towards the women and Ryans, who was not dressed as a priest, walked up to them and asked for directions to Rutland Square (known today as Parnell Square).[3] The women obliged and the couple then turned into nearby Granby Place and out onto Rutland Square. Turning right would have brought them back towards Parnell Street and the city centre. However, they turned left and headed north along Granby Row, a short street of Georgian houses, and on through the junction of Dorset Street. Ahead of them was Saint Mary's Chapel of Ease, known locally as the Black Church. Both Ryans and Mary Kate were talking in an agitated manner and the three women – who had continued to follow the couple – noticed that Mary Kate was visibly upset as she held baby Rose in her arms at all times.

The couple spent time aimlessly walking back and forth in the evening mist, at one stage crossing over Mountjoy Street before immediately crossing back again. Doubling back on their route, the priest and his housekeeper finally arrived at Saint Mary's Place.

Unbeknownst to the preoccupied couple, the three neighbours from the Lower Dominick Street tenements had continued to follow them at a distance all this time. Dublin streets were lit by gas at the time and the dim glow meant the city was in virtual darkness on a winter's evening. However, all three would later testify in court that they watched as the couple stopped and the young woman placed the tiny bundle she was carrying at the doorstep of one of the cottages on the street directly opposite the Black Church.

Following this, the pair moved into the middle of the street and Ryans looked around, as if to see if anyone was about. He then placed a paper parcel next to baby Rose as she lay on the footpath. The two then turned and walked away. They headed in the direction of the nearby Broadstone railway station, the terminus of the train back to Leitrim and the same station where Rita Muldoon had arrived in the city just a few weeks before.

This was surely not the outcome that Mary Kate had been hoping for. As she was taken with her baby by Ryans and walked through the wet streets of Dublin city, she could not have imagined that the pay-off for her silence around the pregnancy and birth of her daughter would be for baby Rose to be abandoned on the side of the street.

Just as the couple 'were walking away nicely as if they never owned the baby', Mrs Ball shouted to her friend Mrs

O'Brien to pick up the child.[4] Mrs Ball, the obvious leader of the trio, called for help. Two men appeared and, after a brief discussion with Mrs Ball, stood in the way of the couple, stopping them from reaching the station.

As a crowd began to gather, Ryans turned and appealed to Mrs O'Brien to give him the child, which she refused to do. Instead, she took baby Rose with her to Fennellys, a tobacconist's shop around the corner on Bolton Street, and used the phone there to call the police. The other women gathered up the paper parcel, which had broken apart on the wet footpath. It was filled with baby clothes. The crowd began to grow larger as evening devotions had just finished at the nearby Saint Saviour's church.

Before the police at the station had a chance to respond to the call, Constable James Murphy, who had been on duty that evening around nearby Rutland Square, heard the commotion from the gathering crowd and made his way to the scene. It was now sometime after 8 p.m. A group of people surrounded the accused couple, who were standing against the wall of one of the cottages. Mary Kate, a vulnerable young woman from a tiny village in rural Ireland, found herself with her back literally to the wall, surrounded by a large crowd on a dark city street in a most awful situation.

After being given an account of what had happened by the locals, the constable took Ryans and Mary Kate into custody. The couple themselves had said nothing and he brought them to the Bridewell, a police station and detention centre nearby.[5]

The baby was taken from the scene by Catherine O'Brien and brought to the Dominican Fathers' vestry in Dominick Street.[6] From there, arrangements were made for baby Rose to be taken into care. She was eventually brought to Pellets-town on the Navan road (later known as Saint Patrick's Guild, one of the largest institutions for the care of children in the country).

At the Bridewell, Ryans and Mary Kate were interviewed by Inspector James O'Gorman of the Dublin Metropolitan Police. He informed them that he was carrying out an investigation into the abandonment of an infant at St Mary's Place and that he intended to charge them.[7] The couple said nothing in response.

If Mary Kate had been upset and distraught earlier in the evening, the scene unfolding before her at the Bridewell must have traumatised her. Her baby was gone, and any hopes of a future with her daughter were turning into a nightmare of criminal charges, detention and a court appearance.

After Inspector O'Gorman had read the charges and cautioned them both, Fr Ryans put forward an explanation that he had been simply helping his young housekeeper to bring the baby to the Dominick Street church so the child could be looked after and, because devotions were going on, this had proven to be impossible. This was Ryans' first offer of an explanation of the circumstances of the abandonment. It would not be his last.

***

The following day, the women who had confronted the couple appeared before Mr E. A. Collins, a magistrate at Inns Quay Police Court, to provide witness statements to the events, as did Constable Murphy and Inspector O'Gorman. The parcel, its paper wrapping opened by the wet ground on which it was laid, was now produced and the baby clothes for Rose were displayed in court as evidence.

The women were very clear in their evidence at this point: that the defendant, Ryans, was present and took a full part in the abandonment. Christina O'Brien stated:

> The male deft. [defendant] was along with the female deft. when she put down the baby. He was beside her and both walked away together.[8]

Mary Dalton testified:

> The female deft. left the child down on a doorstep and the male deft. left a parcel down beside the child. They crossed over the road to turn around to the left to go up by the Broadstone.[9]

The couple were clearly together and the witnesses saw exactly what had happened. Inspector O'Gorman, in his statement to the court, reported that Ryans offered him this explanation of the circumstances:

> … that the man she accused of being the father of the child

was a worthless fellow, that he would not provide a home for anyone and that marriage with him was out of the question and that he was a friend of his own familys [*sic*].

He said that was why he took an interest in the case, that he provided lodgings and paid expenses for three months for the girl in Dublin and when this thing occurred (the bearing of the child) they were on their way to see the clergy in Dominick Street as to its disposal. He said they were at Dominick St. Chapel but devotions were on.[10]

The inspector's account suggests that what Ryans said under questioning had a callous air to it.

It is clear to see why the inspector may have had difficulty accepting Ryans' explanation. Why did he and Mary Kate not wait until devotions ended? He would later make the excuse that 'obviously I could not bring her into a hotel'.[11] The women of Lower Dominick Street testified that a crowd from the devotions gathered shortly after baby Rose was abandoned, so they wouldn't have had long to wait for the Dominican Fathers to become available.

The abandoning of infants in doorways or on the steps of churches, although unusual, was not unheard of in a city like Dublin in the early 1920s. A crime of this nature carried out by a priest in this manner, however, was a very different matter. The formal charge laid against Ryans and his young housekeeper at the City Sessions Court on 16 February 1923 was 'conspiracy to abandon child and abandoning child'.

The young mother had stuck to the name Kate Brown

when arrested and she was charged in that name. She made no statement to Inspector O'Gorman before or after being charged. The only account of her actions was made by Ryans, again in his statement to Inspector O'Gorman. In what must have been an answer to a question, possibly from Ryans' legal representative, the inspector refuted a claim that Mary Kate had disobeyed Ryans after being instructed to wait for him while he made arrangements at the chapel on Dominick Street:

> He [Ryans] didn't say anything about telling the girl to wait for him while he went to Dominick Street Chapel, nor did he say the girl ran after him.[12]

The inspector's account would suggest that contradictions were being noticed in Ryans' story even at this early stage.

CHAPTER 5

Early on 16 February Rita Muldoon's investigation into Fr Ryans appeared to bear some fruit. She received what she says was an important letter in the post with information about Ryans' activities in the Fenagh area of South Leitrim. Unfortunately this letter is no longer extant and Rita doesn't mention what exactly he was supposed to have done; it is also difficult to be sure whether the letter was in response to the enquiries Rita had been making to the military, or if it came from a civilian source. But whatever the source and content, she regarded this letter as highly significant. Despite seeming like a positive development at the time, however, this letter would result in Rita suffering a life-changing betrayal.

What's more, her investigations had not gone unnoticed. That same day Fr Ryans arrived at Dromod station, after spending three days in jail and having been formally charged with the abandonment of Rose. Ryans was met at Dromod station by a Mr Duignan, who told Ryans that Rita had been making enquiries about him. Duignan, who was clearly a supporter of Ryans, also revealed to the priest the contents of the letter Rita Muldoon had received that very day. The anti-Treaty intelligence network had sources working within the postal system at the time and their interception and reading of the letter was entirely possible.

Ryans' behaviour from this point on would reveal a deeply erratic and dangerous character. As he now saw it, Rita had continued to interfere in his personal business in spite of his previous warning.

Following his conversation with Duignan at Dromod railway station, a furious Ryans headed straight to Mohill. There, he sought out Paddy Muldoon, and when he found the doctor, he swore vengeance on Rita for meddling in his affairs.[1] Even though Fr Ryans had just threatened his wife, Paddy arranged for the angry priest to be driven the eight miles from Mohill to the curate's residence in Aughavas, in a car belonging to Delany, a local solicitor. The car was driven by a man named Lyons. Paddy did not tell his wife about this threat until two weeks later. Perhaps he did not want to worry her.

Four days later, on 20 February, Bishop Hoare called to visit the wayward priest at Aughavas. Without hesitation, the bishop suspended him from his position as curate and ordered Ryans to make arrangements to vacate his parish residence.[2]

By now the bishop would have known of Ryans' arrest and the circumstances of the latest trouble his insubordinate priest had become involved in. What is less clear is who might have told Hoare about the pregnancy. It could well have been a concerned Dr Muldoon, possibly through his friendship with Canon Masterson, the local parish priest. But others also knew of at least some of the circumstances, and there were many people who disapproved of Ryans' activities. In any case, Ryans' situation had finally come to the attention of Bishop Hoare, whose patience was at an end.

Fr Ryans was devastated by the bishop's decision, but he was also angry and in no hurry to leave the area.

A week later, on 27 February, Rita Muldoon read the deposition taken in a Dublin court relating to the child abandonment charges laid against Ryans and Mary Kate Gallogly, details of the police investigation into the incident having finally reached South Leitrim. Access for Rita to the deposition most likely came through Paddy, who, as the dispensary doctor for the area in which the young mother lived, was likely to have been questioned about what he knew of her situation. He may even have been called as a witness.

After reading the contents of the deposition, Rita noted in her account that 'I had my eyes opened.'[3] She wrote this in inverted commas. The deposition she read contained the sworn statements of the witnesses to the incident, the arresting policeman and the officer who charged them. Rita read how the witnesses followed the couple and observed the abandonment of the infant; that the young mother had said nothing on arrest or after being charged. She would also have seen how Ryans, after he was charged, maintained that the father of the child was a worthless fellow. This explanation that Ryans put forward in Dublin, and his behaviour in the weeks before the child's birth, must have left Rita Muldoon in no doubt of the priest's character.

In the early days of March, Paddy Muldoon finally told his wife about his meeting with Ryans two weeks earlier and the threats made against her. Paddy also told Rita about Ryans' meeting with Duignan at Dromod station. Rita learned from Lyons, the driver of the solicitor's car that day, about another dangerous incident involving the priest. Rita's own account of what happened tells us: 'From another person named Lyons I also learned ... that Dr Muldoon on the 16th February sent Delany's motor car to convey R to his home in Aughavas.' However, Ryans somehow persuaded the driver to make a slight diversion and take him to Pope's pub in Cloone.

Rita goes on: 'R. turned into Pope's of Cloone and got drunk and fought with the proprietor of house[,] afterwards went home vowing to get his rifle and come back to shoot Pope. However when Fr. R. left the motor and entered curates [*sic*] house Lyons moved the car and came away at top speed (without R).'[4]

Luckily for all concerned, Lyons left Ryans to sober up.

As a result, Rita paid even closer attention to Ryans' movements over the following days as he went on another drunken binge, this time in Mohill. The binge lasted from Saturday 3 March, through Sunday, into Monday 5 March.[5]

Ryans' violent behaviour while drinking was a source of ever increasing concern to her. He appeared to carry two revolvers with him during his three-day binge, and wasn't slow to produce them. On the Saturday evening, he threatened another publican, a Mr Gallagher, to force him to provide more drink, before the publican finally succeeded in throwing the priest out of his premises. Then, at about one o'clock on Sunday morning, Ryans approached three men in Mohill by the names of Rowley, Powell and Clark, and held a revolver to Rowley's face. Rita didn't discover exactly where Ryans spent the rest of that Sunday, but local pubs Brownes and Bradys in Mohill were suggested to her.

She became so concerned at Fr Ryans' erratic actions – worried, perhaps, that he would wind up at their door, revolver in hand – that she approached the military in Mohill on Sunday evening, telling them that he was in the town in an armed and dangerous condition. While it might seem unusual to approach the military about a drunken, out-of-control priest, with no civil police force operating in the area, this was her only option. Inexplicably, they took no action in response to her request to have Ryans disarmed.

It wasn't until Monday evening, 5 March, when a Mr Brady, one of the worried publicans in the town, asked the military to intervene, that they finally responded and got involved – although it was in an unusually restrained fashion, whereby the military removed Ryans from Brady's pub, placed him in his own car and allowed him to drive away from Mohill in the direction of Cloone and Aughavas.[6]

One thing is certain: the response of the National Army to Ryans' behaviour in this three-day period and the priest's own belief in his ability to carry weapons without the normal consequences were troubling.

Ryans appears to have lain low in the following days, as Rita reports no further drunken behaviour on his part. She was aware that he was moving between Aughavas and his family home in Keadue, just over the county border in Roscommon, during this period. She also learned that he had moved some of his possessions from the Aughavas curate's residence to a nearby house belonging to a Mrs Flynn, but had not yet surrendered the key.[7]

Rita likely knew that Ryans would not lie low for long.

***

Ryans was not the only priest Rita had an issue with at this time. On Wednesday 7 March she confronted Fr Edward Dunne after Mass at Fenagh, where he served as a curate.[8] Fr Dunne had been at the meeting at Fr Deniston's in Cloone where Edward Ryans had produced an automatic pistol. The letter received by Rita on 16 February contained information about something relating to Ryans that had happened in Fenagh, the small village where Fr Dunne lived. Now she told the young curate what she had learned from her husband about Duignan's revelations to Fr Ryans at Dromod station and accused him of breaching her confidence.

She would not have known the letter she received might have been intercepted in the postal system; therefore, it made sense to her that Dunne was the source of some of the information that Duignan had given to Ryans.

However, Edward Dunne protested complete innocence

of the charge and was so convincing that Rita accepted his word. She then revealed to him something else she had learned from her husband connected to Ryans' arrest in Dublin, possibly that Paddy intended to give evidence at the forthcoming trial. What it was she told Fr Dunne is not clear, but as events would later play out, Rita Muldoon would be left in absolutely no doubt that this time Fr Dunne had indeed gone back to Ryans with a full account of their meeting, betraying her and giving Ryans more motivation to take revenge. She later wrote, 'I can have no doubt that D. [Dunne] told all this to R. [Ryans]'.[9] Her initial estimation of Dunne as being an untrustworthy character was borne out with tragic results.[10]

***

Just over a week later, on 14 March, Major General Mac Eoin, as part of an inspection of his garrisons in Leitrim and Longford, visited Mohill. The Mohill garrison was based in St Patrick's, a large family home commandeered by the army on the main street, a little way down from the Catholic church at the top of the town. Mac Eoin found the accommodations for his troops in reasonable shape, but he was conscious that they were in the awkward position of having to combine military duties and civil police work in the absence of the Civic Guard. During the visit, Mac Eoin took a note of two buildings he considered suitable to house the Civic Guard: the courthouse and the old RIC barracks.[11]

Rita Muldoon's account of Ryans' earlier behaviour would suggest that the garrison was not performing its basic military duties efficiently. This failure to act could have been part of the known reluctance of pro-Treaty forces in the Leitrim and neighbouring areas to properly get to grips with their former comrades on the anti-Treaty side. This had been scathingly referred to at the highest level the previous month when Minister for Defence and Chief of Staff of the Free State Army Richard Mulcahy remarked on it in the Dáil.[12]

It is likely, in fact, that Mac Eoin's inspection during March of his Longford and Leitrim garrisons was in direct response to his superior's earlier criticisms of the security situation in his command area. Unfortunately there would not be sufficient time to introduce a Civic Guard presence into Mohill before a civilian lay dying on the steps of the courthouse, one of the very buildings Mac Eoin suggested as being suitable to house it.

CHAPTER 6

Rita Muldoon was clearly troubled by what she heard about Fr Edward Ryans' behaviour during the first week of March 1923. But nothing could have prepared her for what was to come on the night of 18 March.

It was a regular Sunday night, apart from it being Passion Sunday, two weeks before Easter. There had been a series of frosty nights earlier that week, but Sunday had been a reasonably warm and sunny day with little or no breeze. Spring was returning slowly to Mohill.

Dr Paddy Muldoon played cards every Sunday night and this night was no different. Paddy's playing companions were the local parish priest, Canon Michael Masterson, and a town official, Edward Geelan. Geelan was clerk of the Mohill Union and Rural District Council, an important position in the town. Forty years older and a distant relative through marriage, he was a good friend of the doctor.[1] Canon Masterson had come to Mohill in 1922, having spent most of his career in St Mel's College, Longford, the school attended by Edward Ryans.[2] The Sunday night card game took place, as it usually did, at Masterson's, beside Saint Patrick's Catholic church at the top of the town.

Sometime after ten o'clock the game finished, and Paddy Muldoon and Edward Geelan walked down through the town together.[3] It was a mostly clear, but moonless night. Street lighting was something of a rarity in country towns around this time, but in the early years of the century Mohill had been one of the first to establish a system of electric street lighting.[4] This meant that both men were visible from a distance.

The two friends made their way down along Bridge Street, no doubt chatting about the affairs of the day, possibly even discussing the ongoing, difficult security situation in the area, which was far from resolved. They would have passed the temporary barracks in St Patrick's, the house that had been taken over by the National Army and had been inspected by Major General Mac Eoin just four days earlier. Inside, there was a small posting of troops whose task was to ensure the safety of the people of the town and its surroundings. Once again, they were about to be found wanting.

The doctor and the district clerk strolled down to the bottom of the street, to the bridge at which they would say farewell for the evening. As they stood together on the footpath a figure stepped from the shadows, raised a rifle to his shoulder and aimed at Dr Muldoon. The gunman was at very close quarters, no more than a couple of yards from them.

The crack of the first rifle shot would have been deafening at such close range. When the shot missed its target, Paddy Muldoon cried out 'Don't shoot', before jumping off the footpath and onto the road. There was no cover nearby and nowhere to run. Edward Geelan also shouted, 'Don't shoot, it is Dr Muldoon.'[5]

The gunman turned off the footpath, away from Geelan, and fired again at the doctor, who was by now in the centre of the road. Simultaneously, from near the courthouse, another gunman fired a shot in the direction of the doctor. Paddy Muldoon, stranded in the middle of the road with fire coming at him from two directions, fell to the ground on his face. He called out to his companion, 'Edward, I am shot.' The two gunmen, with a third accomplice, all wearing trench coats, ran off to the southeast, in the direction of the local railway station.[6]

Edward Geelan went to his fallen friend's side and tried to lift him. Paddy was by now bleeding profusely. At seventy years of age, and with an existing heart condition, Geelan couldn't lift his mortally wounded friend from the road. Instead he ran to a nearby house, the home of Thomas McManus, and banged on the door to get the occupants' attention. McManus' son came to Geelan's aid and helped lift Paddy as far as the courthouse steps, just yards from where he had been shot. Young McManus then ran off to get a priest and a doctor.[7]

Dr Redahan, medical officer of Mohill Union Infirmary, arrived shortly afterwards with Fr Clancy, the local curate, and both men attended the doctor and tried their best to save him. Despite their best efforts, his injuries were too severe. Paddy Muldoon died within minutes of their arrival.

***

Rita was utterly distraught when her husband's lifeless body was carried into their home on a makeshift stretcher, an old door put to a use for which it was never intended.[8] Fr Clancy, who had attended to Paddy at the scene, had gone ahead to break the news to Rita and try to prepare her for the shock of her beloved husband's arrival.[9] But nothing could have prepared her for the sight before her, as blood seeped from Paddy's clothing and pooled on the floor when the bearers laid the stretcher down.

Paddy and Rita's three-and-a-half-year-old daughter, Olwyn, would later recall the image of her dead father being carried into the house. She never forgot seeing his body being placed on the floor of his own surgery.[10] His suit jacket was open, showing a shirt heavily bloodstained from a bullet wound just below his collarbone.

The Muldoon's young housekeeper, Kate Kerr, took the children away to their bedrooms and tried as best she could to comfort them as the enormity of the tragedy unfolded. Rita sat long into the night in the company of Fr Clancy. The priest tried his best to bring some comfort to the grieving widow and her young family.

Even then, amid her fresh grief, Rita was trying to make sense of what had just happened. Her written recollections of 18 March, the night Paddy was murdered, begin with the stark comment: 'Passion Sunday at 11 oc p.m. [*sic*] Dr Muldoon murdered'.[11] She also recorded how gunfire had been heard outside Mohill earlier that evening, how groups of strangers had been sighted in the town that night, and the possible escape route taken by her husband's murderers. Rita noted that the tragic news of her husband's killing was broken to her at 11.30 p.m. by Fr Clancy.

Immediately upon hearing the terrible news, it had flashed across her mind that Fr Edward Ryans was somehow behind the deadly attack. Rita informed Fr Clancy of her conviction later that night.[12]

Had her enquiries enraged Ryans enough to commit murder? She already knew he was a volatile character who had, just a month previously, been relieved of his priestly duties by Bishop Hoare, and, a few days before that, been charged with abandonment of a child. Had the additional information she had given Fr Dunne about what she knew of the abandonment also made its way back to Ryans? These thoughts were no doubt on Rita's mind as she sat in the surgery of Coolebawn House, the dispensary clinic she helped Paddy run.

Her mind must have been in turmoil, their plans and dreams for their future and that of their three – soon to be four – children now ruined. However, the seeds of determination may also have been planted that night, to bring the perpetrator of this awful crime to justice.

***

News of the death of Dr Paddy Muldoon flashed around the world that night. It appeared as a few lines in newspapers from London to Sydney, Toronto, New York and San Francisco. Among the readers of the reports in the California newspapers would have been Paddy's older siblings, who lived on the west coast of the United States. Thomas, a fire brigade officer, was ten years older than Paddy; James, a policeman, was older by seven years; and Joseph, who was in farming, was six years older than Paddy. There was also their sister Roseanne, who was five years older. Their pride in having a doctor in the family was now shattered, replaced by grief at the loss of their youngest brother.

The first official report on the murder of Paddy Muldoon was submitted by Lieutenant M. Keane from the National Army barracks in Mohill to his superior, Captain Sexton.[13] Although it is dated 18 March, it would appear that it was typed in the early hours of the following morning. The officer gives the time of the shooting as about 10.45 p.m., a little earlier than other reports. The lieutenant's short account of the actual attack must have been obtained from Edward Geelan, as it is similar to the version the town clerk would give later at the inquest.

Lieutenant Keane goes on to say that although he didn't have a patrol out in Mohill that evening, he believed that the assailants had been hanging around the town unchallenged, looking out for Dr Muldoon. Some of Keane's men had passed through the town on their way to the barracks at various times up to 10 p.m. Then, around 10.15 p.m., another of them reported that there were 'men kicking about the station, with trench coats on'. Keane immediately sent Sergeant McGuire and another man, both in civilian clothes, in the direction of the station, to see if the suspicious individuals were still in the area. Keane's men didn't see anyone and they had just returned to the barracks when 'a shot was heard in the direction of the station'.

As Keane was arranging for seven of his men, armed with rifles, to investigate, they received the news that Dr Muldoon had been shot. The lieutenant's report went on to suggest a possible motive for the shooting. 'My belief about the case is that he was shot over a prisoner we have here from Glebe, named Doherty. This is the sick man I wrote you about.'

Keane didn't give any details to explain or support his belief, and the man he referred to did not feature in any subsequent inquiries. This was to be the only occasion that anyone in authority set down in writing a possible motive for Paddy Muldoon's murder.

CHAPTER 7

The body of Paddy Muldoon remained at Coolebawn House for a number of days. On 19 March, less than twenty-four hours after the shooting, a post-mortem examination and inquest were held in the Muldoon family home. A jury of twelve (all male) gathered at the house to hear evidence to establish a cause of death. They were tasked with nothing more than the where, how and when of the death; not to establish why he was killed or who exactly might have been responsible.

Various medical personnel and military, clerical and civilian witnesses were summoned, and the Muldoon family home, having served already as a temporary morgue, was abruptly turned into a coroner's courtroom. The report of the post mortem is plain but stark:

Doctor K Delaney:

'In conjunction with Doctor Redehan [*sic*], [who had attended Paddy Muldoon at the scene of the killing] on the 19th March I made a post mortem examination on the body of Micheal [*sic*] Patrick Muldoon. I found a bullet wound which severed one of the principal arteries of his neck. His death was due to shock and hemorrhage following the aforesaid wound.'[1]

The cause of death was clear: a single gunshot fired from close range, causing fatal injury. Dr Redahan confirmed his colleague's findings.

The main witness at the inquest was Edward Geelan. He described to those present: 'I was parting with him at the bridge to go to my house, and as we were parting a shot was fired at Dr Muldoon. I saw the person who fired the shot from the rifle. He was about two yards from Dr Muldoon.' However, he did not say if he knew who the person was. 'We were both on the footpath at the time. No warning was given before the shot was fired. Doctor Muldoon said "Don't shoot" and jumped off the footpath onto the road. I shouted "Don't shoot; it is Dr. Muldoon."' The gunman then turned and fired at the doctor and simultaneously a second gunman also fired at him.

It was evident to the older man, even in that fearful situation, that the attack was not aimed at him but at his companion. He goes on: 'It was quite obvious they knew that Dr Muldoon was there … The doctor then fell on his face about five yards from where he was standing when he was first fired at, and said "Edward, I am shot."'

Geelan recounted that the two gunmen and a third associate, all wearing trench coats, immediately ran from the area in the direction of the railway station as soon as they saw that Paddy Muldoon had been hit. He described his own and the others' efforts in trying to help Paddy, whom they could see was badly wounded, and how he was there when the young doctor passed away.[2]

The evidence Edward Geelan gave at the inquest was factual and unemotional. It is likely that he may still have been in shock, so soon after witnessing at close quarters the murder of his young friend. He never recovered from the trauma, and his experiences that awful night affected him for the rest of his life.[3]

The issue of how well lit this part of the town was would later become a crucial factor in the story. Rita Muldoon mentioned in a letter to the press the following year: 'It was further disclosed at the inquest that the night was bright and that a street light was close by.'[4]

Fr Clancy was the last of four witnesses to testify. He stated that young McManus called to his house at 11.30 p.m. and told him that Paddy Muldoon was seriously injured. He went immediately to the doctor's assistance. Fr Clancy continued: 'He was alive when I arrived and I administered the Sacraments to him.' This must have been some comfort to Rita, his widow, and to all of Paddy's relations.

The National Army was represented at the inquest by Lieutenant Keane. This was just a few hours after he made his report on the incident. Also present were an Inspector Breen and Sergeant Collins from the Civic Guards who had come, like some of the other officials, from the county town of Carrick-on-Shannon for the proceedings.

The jury accepted the evidence as presented and returned a verdict that the thirty-one-year-old Dr Michael Patrick Muldoon 'was wilfully murdered by a person or persons unknown'.[5]

In her written account of the inquest, Rita Muldoon recorded how her husband's murder had been accurately described. The fact that the verdict returned used the term murder was particularly important to her. Her kind and loving husband had been murdered. Now she just wanted to know for sure who had done it.

***

On the morning of 20 March, the day following the inquest, with her husband's remains still in the house, Rita arranged for Mass to be offered in the family home. At breakfast, after the Mass, she learned from general conversation that Fr Ryans had been observed driving through Fenagh and on to Aughavas on the night of her husband's murder.[6] Motor cars were rare enough in rural Ireland at that time, so they would be instantly noticed. Just two days after the shooting Rita was already picking up information that might assist in bringing those she felt were the perpetrators to justice.

The funeral Mass took place in St Patrick's church, Mohill on Wednesday 21 March. Canon Masterson, the man who had played cards with Paddy on the night of his murder, officiated at the Mass, and Fr Clancy assisted him. While there was a large turnout of clergymen from neighbouring parishes and further afield, neither Fr Edward Ryans nor Fr Edward Dunne are listed as being in attendance.[7]

The very Rev. Canon Masterson paid an eloquent tribute to his deceased friend in front of the St Patrick's congregation. He described him as a skilled and brilliant doctor and an exemplary and devout Catholic. The canon asked the congregation to pray for Dr Muldoon, whom he said was not murdered but butchered.[8] The funeral was attended by a large number of people who were keen to express their sympathy to Paddy Muldoon's family, as well as their abhorrence of this cruel murder. Paddy and his family had lived in the town for five years; he had been highly regarded as a dedicated doctor and was very popular in the area.

Up to this point Rita Muldoon had only mentioned her suspicion about Ryans' involvement in her husband's murder to Fr Clancy and to another clergyman, Fr John Pinkman, who had been a curate in Mohill up to the previous November.[9] During the course of the funeral, however, Rita was surprised to learn that most of the people present shared her suspicions about what had happened. Everyone that the grieving widow spoke to, as she wrote herself, was 'full of the terrible subject'. When Frank, an older brother of Paddy, spoke with Fr John Pinkman on the day of the funeral, Fr Pinkman said to him: 'Frank, I believe it was Fr Ryans shot him.'[10]

Indeed, Rita's belief was echoed many times at the funeral that day, the perception being that the popular young doctor's murder was directly connected to his knowledge of Ryans' affairs and Mary Kate's pregnancy. From then on Rita no longer felt the need to keep her suspicions to herself.[11]

After the funeral Mass in Mohill, a large cortège followed the coffin of the young father on his final journey to the

Muldoon family burial ground at the old Abbey in Fenagh, seven miles north of the town, where his remains were laid to rest.[12]

A few days after the funeral, on 24 March, a poignant and heartfelt article about the doctor appeared in the *Roscommon Herald*. The headline read:

Popular Mohill Doctor Shot Dead

No motive known

The late Dr Muldoon – Loss to the community

The body of the article contained an extraordinary level of praise for the young doctor:

> The terrible occurrence has filled everyone in Mohill and South Leitrim with horror. To say that Dr. Muldoon was immensely popular would be but a poor and bare way indeed to express the feelings of affection and esteem in which he was held throughout South Leitrim, in the adjoining counties and everywhere he was known.

There follows a testimonial of almost heroic proportions:

> He came to Mohill with a great reputation for medical skill which was soon proved out by fact, but added to this, there was that which was equally valuable, his great human qualities, his innate courtesy and kindness, his imperturbable affability and

geniality, and a nature in which tone or airs or considerations of class distinction found absolutely no part. With him, the poor were as much at home as the rich, the simple and the educated. Indeed he was veritably the poor man's friend, and what his death means to the poor of a very large area can only later be estimated. At any hour, night or day, in storm or in sunshine, he was ready to start out on their call and his attendance was not a mere cursory business but he would stay on and do all that was possible at the time and devote all possible attention to the case afterwards. His services really came into prominence during the influenza epidemic a few years ago and he established a great name for himself as an expert in the treatment of pneumonia.

The newspaper article was careful not to speculate on what might have been behind the attack:

No motive for the crime can be conceived. That the assailants knew it was Dr. Muldoon is obvious, but what the reason was is not even conjecture. During the Anglo-Irish war, Dr. Muldoon was a Sinn Feiner. Since the split, he took no sides in the Irish struggle and an uncharitable word towards anybody was never heard from his mouth.

***

Rita's immediate prospects after the loss of her husband were precarious to say the least. There was no widow's pension in Ireland at this time, so she had no source of income and she had three young children to support and a fourth on the way.

Shortly after the funeral, a number of Dr Muldoon's medical colleagues set about organising a national collection to assist Rita and the children in their difficult financial predicament. Dr Tom Reynolds, one of the main organisers, wrote from Ballinamore on 2 April 1923 to Rita's brother, Ambrose, to advise him of the arrangements he was making.[13] The collection would be aimed at the public in general and the medical profession in particular. The intention was that Canon Masterson would be appointed treasurer, and Dr Reynolds and Dr Charles Dolan of Ballinamore would act as secretaries. Dr Reynolds was arranging to have a notice or memorial drafted, and for hundreds of copies to be printed and distributed, and he undertook to forward fifty to one hundred copies to Ambrose.

Dr Reynolds' letter then referred to 'Hennessy's suggestion that we should state in the memorial that the motive for the murder was that Paddy refused to issue a certificate not in accordance with facts'. This hints again that the motive for the murder could have been connected to Paddy's medical duties, in this case a refusal to certify Mary Kate Gallogly for involuntary admission to an asylum. This would have prevented her from appearing in court on the abandonment charge.[14] However, Reynolds himself felt 'that there were all kind of rumours going around, some of which impute motives quite different'. His own belief was that the best thing to do was simply state that Paddy Muldoon 'was cruelly murdered without the slightest warning and with premeditation'.

As it transpired, neither Hennessy's suggestion nor Reynolds' own proposal were included in the final printed appeal, which appeared in the national press in April 1923, and later in other publications.[15] The appeal does provide an insight into the case, however:

AN APPEAL

On Behalf Of
THE WIFE AND INFANT FAMILY OF
The Late Dr. PATRICK MULDOON, MOHILL

The tragic murder of Dr. Muldoon at the early age of 31 years has shocked the public even at a time when such events are unfortunately not infrequent, but the full poignancy of the sad event is only realised by those who know what his untimely demise means to his afflicted wife, left with a helpless family. Dr. Muldoon had hardly begun his professional life, and his skill, combined with a generous and open-hearted personality, was promising a brilliant career, when his untimely death intervened to cut it short.

It is hardly necessary to point out that Dr. Muldoon had not had the time or opportunity to provide for his dependents in the unforeseen circumstances that have befallen. His widow has three children – the eldest only four years old – for whom to provide. To his friends, therefore, we appeal with confidence. We know they will show their appreciation of his excellent qualities, and their sympathy with Mrs. Muldoon and her helpless family. To his medical brethren and the general public to whom Dr. Muldoon was less known, we appeal with scarcely less confidence.

Their sympathy has not been denied to his widow, and we venture to think that very many will be glad to take this opportunity of giving that sympathy practical expression.

Subscriptions may be sent to any of the undersigned, and will be acknowledged by publication in the local and medical Press.

Very Rev. M. CANON MASTERSON, P.P.
(Mohill, Co. Leitrim), Treasurer

CHARLES DOLAN, L.R.C.S.E.
THOMAS REYNOLDS, M.B.
(Ballinamore, Co. Leitrim), Secretaries.[16]

The wording suggested by Tom Reynolds for the appeal was not totally overlooked, however. Rita Muldoon would later have an imposing white marble headstone erected over her husband's grave. It is engraved with the words:

IN UNDYING MEMORY OF MY BELOVED HUS-BAND PADDY (Dr M.P. MULDOON) WHO WAS CRUELLY MURDERED AT MOHILL, Co. LEITRIM, 18th March 1923

The appeal by Paddy Muldoon's medical colleagues raised about £500, which helped Rita over her immediate financial worries. In the years ahead, however, she would have a longer and more difficult experience trying to claim compensation for what had been done to her husband.

In the meantime, Rita was clearly looking at other avenues to raise money for her family. On 5 April, the same day that the Mohill-based *Leitrim Advertiser* carried a comprehensive report on Dr Muldoon's funeral, it also carried a notice of a public auction to be held in Mohill the following day. The sale of 'A residue of Household Furniture' and 'Outdoor Effects' included a 'surgical couch, writing desk, a five-seater Ford Touring car, a Douglas motor bicycle as well as an in-calf cow', and these items were advertised 'on the instructions of the Representatives of the late Dr M.P. Muldoon'.[17] There was no reference to the sale of Coolebawn House, however, which suggests that it was a rented property.

Rita was forced to make some very quick decisions in the weeks following her husband's death. The grieving widow was moving back to be near her own family, the Lees in Clifden, County Galway, as she faced into the birth of her fourth child. Her young housekeeper, Kate Kerr, was deeply saddened by the events and the family's impending departure. The opportunities Paddy and Rita had given her, including the possibility of providing the means and encouragement to obtain a recognised qualification, were now no longer available. On a more personal note, she was upset that she might never see the children again.[18]

Most likely, Rita's decision was brought about by the need to get away from Mohill itself, where she would be permanently reminded of her husband's murder as she went about her daily life in the small town. However, while she was keen to quickly leave the area with her young family, Rita would prove tenacious in the following years in defending Paddy's memory and seeking justice for her dead husband.

CHAPTER 8

Paddy Muldoon's nephew, Thomas William Muldoon, was two months short of his eighth birthday when his uncle was murdered. Thomas William's father, Frank, was an older brother of Paddy's. The events made a lasting impression on Thomas William and as he went through life he became something of a crusader for justice on behalf of his uncle.

Some years later, Thomas William managed to locate and take possession of what appears to be at least part of the police file on the Muldoon case. It consists of letters copied into a ledger in the same handwriting, and a series of typewritten reports from some of those involved in the investigation.[1] The file shows how limited the original inquiry was and, conversely, how much attention the case was given at the highest level in the Irish government in the months that followed.

The earliest item in the file is a letter dated 20 March 1923, two days after the murder, from Inspector William Breen of Carrick-on-Shannon, reporting to the superintendent at the regional headquarters in Sligo.[2] Inspector Breen had attended the inquest and his account of the shooting seems to be taken directly from Edward Geelan's testimony, giving the time of the attack as 11 p.m. and the cause of death a shot 'fired into Dr Muldoon's breast'. Dr Redahan, who was present when

Paddy Muldoon died, would later certify the cause of death as 'a result of gunshot wound under right clavicle severing the blood vessels in region & haemorrhage & shock following same'.[3] It appears the bullet entered near the collarbone, severing an artery close to his neck. Breen also confirmed Dr Muldoon was facing his killer when he suffered the fatal wound.

Two days after the funeral, a copy of Inspector Breen's report was forwarded to the commissioner of the Civic Guard, who was based at its headquarters in the Phoenix Park in Dublin. It was accompanied by a further letter, signed by Breen, seeking some directions in the case and providing the additional information that the attackers had tried to gain admittance to Brown's pub in Mohill prior to the shooting.[4] This new information was not obtained by the police themselves but came from a friend of Rita, George Lynch.

Lynch was the state solicitor for Leitrim and had been at the inquest in his official capacity. George's wife, Frances, was one of Rita's friends and George was one of a number of solicitors who helped and advised Rita after Paddy's death.[5] George Lynch appears to have used his time in Mohill to carry out some preliminary enquiries, possibly at Rita Muldoon's request. His office was in Carrick-on-Shannon, where Inspector Breen was also based, and they would have known each other and worked together on occasion.

The written communication from Inspector Breen did not meet with a helpful response from headquarters. Instead, on 26 March, Éamon O'Cugain, otherwise Eamonn (Ned) Coogan, assistant commissioner, sent back a curt reply to say, 'This should have been reported on Form 38 in the first instance. Form 38 should be forwarded by return.'[6] The leading figures in the recently founded Civic Guard seemed more intent on bureaucratic accuracy than on information that would help solve a murder.

A few days later, Superintendent R. Muldoon of Sligo (no relation to the doctor) submitted a fresh report, presumably on the required Form 38. This document, dated 3 April 1923, noted that at the inquest 'no one could throw any light on whom the murderers were or what could be the motive'.[7] It is not clear if what is in the superintendent's report is a result of any information other than the statements made at the inquest. That was to be the last known involvement of the local Civic Guard in the investigation, as it was about to pass into other hands.

***

There was one final entry in Rita Muldoon's diary before she left Mohill for good.[8] The last comment is an optimistic one. It reads, 'On Holy Thursday, 29th [March] in Longford met by chance Major General Mc Keown [*sic*] who declared his determination to have R arrested. R was arrested I think next day.'[9]

In the weeks before her husband's murder, Rita had tried unsuccessfully to get the military in Mohill to do something about Fr Ryans' unlawful behaviour and the threat he posed to her family. Now, nearly two weeks after Paddy's death, it seemed to Rita that Ryans was finally being dealt with, likely as a result of this chance meeting between herself and Major General Mac Eoin.

Coincidentally, on the same day as Rita's encounter with Mac Eoin in Longford, Ryans' younger brother, Vincent, voluntarily surrendered himself to the authorities. Vincent and a man named Francis Duignan, described in the press as leading members of the Arigna column of the anti-Treaty forces, both surrendered their arms to the National Army at Keadue, County Roscommon, late on Holy Thursday.[10]

The Arigna column had been responsible for the attack on the National Army barracks in Ballinamore in early February, the one in which Fr Ryans appears to have played some part, as well as for the murderous attack on Ballyconnell. The National Army's response to the Ballyconnell attack had effectively crushed the power of the anti-Treaty unit.[11] After surrendering and handing in their arms, Vincent Ryans and Francis Duignan were released and permitted to return to their homes.[12]

The very next morning Edward Ryans was arrested at the family home in Keadue and taken to the military barracks in Boyle, County Roscommon.[13] Unlike his brother, the priest was not immediately released.

With Ryans' arrest, Rita Muldoon must have thought there was now a real prospect of justice for her husband's murder. However, it turned out that, although the arrest of Ryans was connected to his role in Paddy's murder, after a few days had passed Ryans was handed into civilian custody. He was transferred to Mountjoy Prison in Dublin to await trial for the abandonment of Rose Brown.[14]

That case was set for 9 May. It would have been reasonable, at the time, for Rita to assume that the suspicion around Ryans' involvement in the murder would have been further reason for his detention and that the murder case would be pursued in tandem with the abandonment trial. After all, Mac Eoin had access to the best intelligence in South Leitrim at that time, as well as having informants and troops on the ground.

And it certainly did appear that progress was being made in the murder investigation. Before Ryans was handed over, Mac Eoin reported to his superior, Minister for Defence Richard Mulcahy, during the early weeks of April.[15] In the report, Mac Eoin explained that he had used his position to find the name of the gunman alleged to have committed the shooting of Paddy Muldoon: the name he was given was that of John Charles Keegan.

Keegan was the anti-Treaty fighter who had defected from the National Army and become involved in various attacks around Leitrim and Longford in the early months of 1923. At least one of those attacks also involved Fr Edward Ryans. Although Mac Eoin doesn't say where he got his information, the report makes it clear that, from descriptions provided by a number of people, Keegan is believed to have been the killer. The doctor's friend and companion on the night, Edward Geelan, may well have been one of those providing a description, though it appears that others were also aware of the identity of the perpetrator.

Following Mac Eoin's report, Mulcahy wrote to Minister for Home Affairs Kevin O'Higgins, the minister in charge of the police. The letter O'Higgins received from the minister for defence quotes a section of Mac Eoin's report of events on the night of the murder:

A/8084

Ministry of Defence
Portobello Barracks
April 16th 1923

Personal & Confidential

The Minister for Home Affairs

A Chara

The following is an extract from a communication dated 10th April from Major Gen. Mc Keon [*sic*] on the Father Ryans case:–

'We cannot get very far with this case yet. On the 18th March – the night of the murder – Father Ryans went up the Fenagh Road in the direction of Aughavas where he stayed for 10 minutes. He went back to Cloone Creamery, where he turned in the direction of Cattan. This is as far as we can trace him yet. The inference is as follows:– A number of men saw three persons who committed the murder. From the description given it is believed that the leader is a man named Keegan who is a native of Cattan, Co. Leitrim. Father Ryans met these fellows in Cattan, picked them up and took them back to Mohill.'

Father Ryans himself maintains that he was in Dublin on this night and that he was not in the locality at all. Inquiries are still proceeding on this case and it will take considerable time to complete them. I would suggest that on the last charge you would send down a few C.I.D. men and report to me here first. I attach report from Captain Carter T.D., and I am enclosing a statement on the matter which accompanied his communication.

Beir Beannacht

(Sgd) R. Ua Maolchatha

Aire Chosanta[16]

This letter, from one minister to another, makes it clear that two of the top members of the Irish Free State government were aware of who was involved and under suspicion in the case. Notable is the fact that the letter doesn't refer to it as the 'Paddy Muldoon case'; instead, it is a preliminary investigation into the murder of a doctor by Fr Edward Ryans, using gunmen associated with the priest.

Even at this early stage the evidence appeared damning. Ryans had means: weapons, transportation and contacts who were well versed in ambushes and other violent activity. Furthermore, he had opportunity, as Paddy Muldoon was not difficult to find, especially on a Sunday night after his weekly card game. Added to that, Mac Eoin puts Ryans close to the scene with Keegan the gunman and two others on the night of 18 March. Perhaps most sinister of all were Ryans' potential motives. He would not have wanted Dr Muldoon present at a court case for the abandonment of Rose Brown, particularly if Paddy could testify as to the parentage of Rose and the approach to commit Mary Kate Gallogly to an asylum. Even more damning, the Muldoon family and others maintain there was a request made by Ryans for Paddy to intervene in the pregnancy of Mary Kate Gallogly and that Paddy's refusal to perform a termination was somehow seen by the priest as the cause of all his troubles now. If that were to be revealed in open court, the priest would be ruined.[17]

Minister for Defence Mulcahy now felt the case warranted the attention of the Dublin-based Criminal Investigation Department (CID), perhaps indicating that he believed there was a need to closely monitor and control the investigation. Sure enough, shortly after receiving this letter, Minister Kevin O'Higgins ordered a team to go to Mohill and get to the bottom of the case.

***

The team who took on the murder investigation was from CID, operating from Oriel House in Dublin. The CID had been set up by Michael Collins after the Truce in 1921. It was initially staffed with many of Collins' IRA intelligence operatives and experienced gunmen, including members of a group known as 'the Squad', the dedicated assassination unit set up by Collins to counter the work of British intelligence during the War of Independence.

The CID was led by Major General Joe McGrath, and its operational commander was Captain Patrick Moynihan, who had been Michael Collins' chief intelligence agent in the mail centre that replaced the General Post Office in Dublin after it was gutted in the 1916 Rising. On Collins' death in August 1922, control of the CID, which was separate from the unarmed Civic Guard, passed to Kevin O'Higgins in his role as minister for home affairs. Individual members of the CID were not slow to turn the methods and experience they had acquired in the War of Independence with the British against their new anti-Treaty republican adversaries. As a result, by April 1923 the CID had gained a reputation for brutal interrogation methods and was reported to have been involved in the unlawful killings of a number of republican prisoners and activists.

While Mulcahy, or for that matter Mac Eoin, had no direct command over the CID, they would have had connections to some of its principal officers from a shared involvement with Michael Collins, and loyalty to the dead leader. Mac Eoin's successes and reputation during the War of Independence had made him a favourite of Collins. Known as the Blacksmith of Ballinalee, Mac Eoin had led a successful defence of Ballinalee against a much larger British force in November 1920. In February 1921 he led the North Longford flying column in a successful ambush at Clonfin, which resulted in the deaths of four members of the British Auxiliary Division. After the Truce, Collins had actually delayed the Treaty negotiations until the British released Mac Eoin from imprisonment in Dublin, where he was being held under sentence of death. Mac Eoin had joined the newly formed National Army and was appointed General Officer Commanding (GOC) of the Western Command.[18]

The choice of the CID to investigate the murder of a civilian in Leitrim seemed an unusual one. The CID mainly operated in the Dublin metropolitan area, so it would appear that there was more at stake in the Mohill killing than there initially appeared to be.

Moynihan picked Superintendent Finian O'Driscoll and Inspector Mooney to travel to South Leitrim to investigate the killing of Paddy Muldoon. These two CID men later claimed that they found it very difficult to obtain any definite information in the locality. They were able to establish, to some extent, the route the three attackers took into Mohill on the night Dr Muldoon was killed. This included an attempt by the gang to gain admittance to Brown's pub in Mohill. However, the publican stuck to the details given in an earlier statement: that he had refused them admittance and could only give a slight description of the culprits. The detectives theorised that the attackers must have been familiar with Dr Muldoon's routine and that he was likely well known to them. They reported that the young doctor was in the habit of visiting Canon Masterson every Sunday evening and on the night of his shooting he left the canon's house with Edward Geelan at the usual time around 11 p.m. and was shot dead within ten minutes on the way back to his home.[19]

The detectives then obtained a statement concerning Fr Ryans' whereabouts on the night of the murder from one Patrick Flynn.[20] The Flynn family were neighbours and friends of Ryans in Aughavas. Ryans had previously told his bishop that he sometimes slept at the Flynns' home while he was on the run during the War of Independence.[21] Bishop Hoare had agreed to that arrangement, possibly because of Mrs Flynn's connections: she had a brother and a half-brother in the priesthood and was herself a relative of the bishop.[22]

Patrick Flynn gave a statement saying that Ryans had driven to their house between 7 and 8 p.m. on the night of 18 March, the night Paddy Muldoon was shot, and had remained there up to 10 p.m. Apparently both the priest and Flynn then left for the nearby house that Ryans previously occupied as curate of Aughavas and returned again to the Flynn house at about 11 p.m. The priest left for Dublin at about 9 a.m. the following morning.

Though this statement may well have been an attempt to provide the priest with an alibi, it was totally at odds with Ryans' earlier claim to Mac Eoin that he wasn't in the area at all on the night of the murder. Therefore, regardless of Flynn's intent, all his statement did was suggest that Ryans was a liar.

Mooney and O'Driscoll managed to detain two men suspected of being part of the murder gang. One was a man named McIntyre of Cattan, Mohill; the other was John Joe McGarry of Clonagher, Mohill. Both were interrogated. McIntyre gave a satisfactory account of his movements on the night of the murder, while McGarry was released when they could find no evidence to justify his detention. The detectives carried out a careful search for the third and main suspect, John Charles Keegan, but were unable to locate him as he was on the run at the time.[23]

Keegan, who had previously been identified by Major General Mac Eoin as the leader of the attackers, had good reason to be on the run. He had been captured under arms by the National Army shortly after he had helped with a mass jail break of anti-Treaty prisoners from Longford Barracks, underwent trial by court martial and was sentenced to execution, but escaped himself before the sentence could be carried out.[24] Having just avoided execution, he was not an obvious choice to participate in the murder of an innocent civilian; however, John Charles Keegan would prove to be no ordinary individual.

These interrogations weren't the end of the CID's involvement in the activities of Fr Edward Ryans. They continued to investigate the murder for another three months. Mooney and O'Driscoll didn't manage to arrest anyone in connection with the crime, but they did report back that 'owing to information at their disposal' they were of the opinion that it might be useful to interview Fr Ryans, who was by then detained in Dublin.[25]

***

The official investigation into Paddy Muldoon's murder wasn't the only action being taken as a result of his untimely death. By the end of March 1923 Rita's brother, Ambrose Lee, a Clifden-based solicitor and barrister, was writing to his friend and fellow solicitor Patrick Hogan. Hogan, like Ambrose, was from Galway and was minister for agriculture in the nascent Free State government. Ambrose was seeking assistance from the minister in obtaining compensation for his recently widowed sister.

The minister initially wrote back to say how appalled he was about Dr Muldoon's case and that he would speak to the president, W. T. Cosgrave, about it immediately to see what could be done.[26] Hogan was also a close friend of the home affairs minister, Kevin O'Higgins. In fact, Hogan lived with O'Higgins and his family in Dublin during the Civil War period.[27] He no doubt kept his fellow minister informed of any information coming to him from Rita's brother.

On 9 April 1923 Minister Hogan wrote again to Ambrose, enclosing a copy of the terms of reference of the Compensation (Personal Injuries) Committee.[28] He instructed Ambrose to get his sister to make an application as soon as possible. He also told him that he had been interceding on Rita Muldoon's behalf and was confident that she would get a fair hearing. In thanking his friend, Ambrose wrote back to Minister Hogan, saying that his sister and young family were left in practical poverty, as Dr Muldoon had not been in practice long enough to make proper financial provision for them. Ambrose also remarked, in reference to his brother-in-law's murder, that he 'could not imagine how a Republic is to be won by such actions'.[29]

CHAPTER 9

One of the stranger things about the chief suspect in this case was that it wasn't the first time he had been suspected of being involved in a murder. One night in December 1920, two men burst into Fr Edward Ryans' house in the dead of night. Both men were masked and were brandishing revolvers. They ransacked the house, then dragged the curate outside, abused him and told him that they had come to shoot him. One of them challenged the priest about the death of Francis Curran, who was murdered nearby the previous April, and also about an attack on Curran's employer, a rate collector.[1] The curate explained that while he had been at the scene of the killing, he was only there to give the last rites, and by the time he arrived Curran was already dead.[2]

The fatal shooting of Francis Curran in April 1920 was the first fatality of the War of Independence in County Leitrim.[3] Curran, aged sixty-eight and from Aughavas, was returning home on the night of 12 April from working with Michael Curran (they were not related), county councillor and rate collector. He was met on the road by two masked men who shot him in the chest with a shotgun at close range.[4] Following this:

The wounded and dying man called to a cyclist who came

upon the scene to go for a priest for him and he cycled to Aughavas – a short distance off – for Fr. Ryan [*sic*]. This was probably the last word the poor man spoke for when Fr. Ryan arrived a short time later at the scene of the tragedy, Curran was dead.[5]

The two masked intruders in Fr Ryans' house demanded that the priest surrender his shotgun to the local barracks. They also insisted that he refund a fine of £110 he had imposed, in his role as a judge in the Sinn Féin courts, on a local individual for giving information to the Royal Irish Constabulary (RIC).

Although the armed and masked men were highly agitated and extremely threatening, Ryans managed to convince them that he couldn't possibly carry out their demands in the middle of the night. They then gave him forty-eight hours to comply and promised to return and carry out the threat to his life if he didn't. Two days later two lorries containing armed crown forces returned to the house, but by then Fr Ryans was on the run. He did not comply with their demands.

The account of this incident is taken directly from Ryans' own correspondence with Bishop Hoare, as well as the RIC Register of Crimes for Connaught for the period July to December 1920. As Ryans went on the run immediately afterwards, we can assume that he did not report the incident to the local authorities and that instead it was reported internally by the raiders, who were likely members of the crown forces in disguise.[6]

The account Ryans gave to the bishop concerning the raid omitted any detail of the two demands they made on him. Ryans' position as a judge in the Sinn Féin courts was already barely tolerated by his bishop. A few months prior to this incident, in September 1920, Bishop Hoare had received an anonymous letter claiming that Ryans' judgements were 'very one-sided and will eventually result in serious consequences'.[7] He would also undoubtedly have been extremely concerned to learn about the curate's possession of a shotgun.

Michael Curran, the local rate collector and employer of the murdered man, was himself shot and slightly injured at his home in Aughavas in October 1920, just over a month prior to the attack on Ryans. There is a strong probability that Michael Curran was the local individual that Ryans had fined for giving information to the constabulary.[8]

In demanding that Ryans surrender his shotgun, while at the same time challenging him about the Curran murder, the intruders would appear to be linking the curate's weapon to the attack. That Ryans kept details of the shotgun from Bishop Hoare, only informing him that 'certain demands' were made on him, is telling. Ryans did, however, tell the bishop that he was challenged in connection with the Curran murder and the separate attack on Curran's employer. He also disclosed to his bishop that both the RIC and the British Army had 'been charging me of involvement in active association with the volunteers', and specifically they branded him 'the leader of the murder gang'.[9]

These accusations, along with the fact that Ryans went on the run, would ordinarily have led to the priest being relieved of his duties at the very least. Ryans did receive a dressing down by letter from Bishop Hoare covering his various misdeeds, involving everything from rebellion to accounting irregularities and poor relations with his fellow priests. But Ryans made an extraordinary series of pleas to his bishop to be allowed to continue in service:

Aughavas
Carrigallen
31st January 1921

My Lord

I beg to be excused from attending the Conference tomorrow. I am sure if I did so I would fall into the hands of the Crown Forces.

Owing to your Lordship's attitude towards the present National movement I did not expect actual sympathy as a result of my letter, but I am very grieved that your Lordship should cast undeserved taunts at me. I certainly do not acknowledge that I am in sin in acting as I have done – playing the part of an Irishman in this seven century old struggle for my country's freedom, a struggle from which the Irish priest was never absent.

As for the part I played in connection with the Republican courts, your Lordship will doubtless recollect that after the last Conference you permitted me to act for a further short period as I had been acting.

As regards my being in conflict with my parish priests – I have never been the aggressor, and as your Lordship will now clearly recollect, in any complaint which my parish priest ever made and which I answered before you I was always easily the victor. Father Dolan, who unlike others is an honourable man, never reported me, nor had he occasion to do so, though his political views were utterly divergent from mine.

I have not been in conflict with Fr. McGivney, though he stated in writing to me, and also announced to the people from the altar that your Lordship directed him to take charge of all the revenues, or dues, of all the parish and that no monies be handed to me. I am gratified to find that he had no authority for doing this. He clearly wants to be in conflict with me. One day I met him walking with Curran the ex-County Councillor, whose family have linked my name so freely and with such impunity with murder and attempted murder, and Fr. McGivney did not – presumably he dared not – raise his eyes to speak to me.

This association of my name with murder was not good, and should not have been permitted to the laity, and the result of that talk I blame largely for the trouble I am now in.

On Saturday evening last – 29th inst. – about 60 police in charge of D.I. Gore-Hickman of Mohill rushed into the house of the teacher of Aughavas School where he evidently suspected I might be staying. He called for the 'murderer' – The teacher asked what was meant by that – the answer was 'murderer Ryans'. This is directly the result of the talk the Curran family were allowed to use.

The police next rushed to my house – terrorised my house-keeper for half an hour in an endeavour to force her to tell where I was – next the District Inspector offered her a bribe of two years' salary if she should tell. When this failed he warned her not to be in the house when next they raid it.

During that night again the Crown forces again [*sic*] searched my house, this time breaking into it. Lest they should raid the Church for me at mass time I did not say a public mass on Sunday.

Whenever I did not say my mass on Sunday or Holyday I always had a priest to take my place.

I trust your Lordship may have patience with me for another short while.

I am more anxious than ever, for my people's sake, to evade arrest – or as I believe shooting. My young brother, a student in Dublin against whom there cannot possibly be any charge, was arrested a week ago and of course he will get at least internment.

I have the honour to remain Your Lordship's obedient servant,

Edward Ryans

This letter shows that Fr Ryans did not feel safe living in his own house, a fact that was undoubtedly compromising his ability to carry out his clerical duties. However, his strong commitment to the republican cause was not shaken by his bishop's disapproval of his involvement in political affairs and the 'undeserved taunts' received from him. Neither was he accepting of being 'in sin' as a result of a probable restating by his superior of the Papal censure for belonging to a revolutionary society. He was as combative as ever in defending his political stance and relationship with his parish superior, Fr McGivney, and also his efforts in the carrying out of his clerical responsibilities in difficult circumstances.

Ultimately, however, Fr Ryans was aware of his dependency on Bishop Hoare for the retention of his position and livelihood in Aughavas. As long as he remained in his clerical position he would have some protection, at least from the more disciplined elements of the crown forces.

The bishop, on the other hand, aware of his curate's strong political views and involvement, must have been wondering exactly what sort of influence Ryans was having on the parish of Aughavas, and if that influence contributed to an atmosphere which saw the killing of Francis Curran, an innocent man. The efforts that the RIC and military were putting in to apprehend him suggest that they believed Ryans was an extremely dangerous enemy of the State. Bishop Hoare must have been concerned about where all this was going to end.

Despite Ryans' request for a further short period of patience, it seems Bishop Hoare had made the decision to replace Ryans as curate in Aughavas. On 11 February 1921 Fr Ryans wrote to his superior in dramatic terms:

> What crime have I committed that you treat me in the manner indicated in your letter. I thought it bad enough to be persecuted by the enemies of our country, but now your lordship threatens to throw me to the wolves.

He went on to say, 'Where will I live, or how am I going to support myself in these difficult times.'[10]

The letter ends with a request for the bishop 'to stay your hand for the present'. Bishop Hoare attached his signed response to the front page of his curate's letter under the date 13 February 1921: 'What can I do, you are now away from your work exactly two months. I can't leave this populous Parish to one priest.'[11]

Ryans appears to have convinced the bishop to change his mind about replacing him in February 1921 as he remained in Aughavas.[12] In his following letter to the bishop, in June 1921, he mentioned that, for safety's sake, he stayed in the house of Mrs Flynn at night and could be easily reached there as it was close to the chapel in Aughavas. This is the same Mrs Flynn at whose home Ryans supposedly stayed on the night of Paddy Muldoon's murder.[13]

The Church authorities had a fine line to walk when dealing with members of the clergy involved in rebellion during the War of Independence. They wanted to be seen to be on the side of the risen people, as it were, but were tempered by a desire to stay on the right side of those officially in power. This might account for some of the bishop's leniency towards Ryans during that time. When the Civil War broke out, however, the Church felt no such constraint and Ryans' change of allegiance, from the pro- to anti-Treaty side, would have provided the bishop with an excuse to get rid of the troublesome priest. And yet, because the bishop didn't take this chance, by the spring of 1923 the rogue priest's actions had the potential to seriously embarrass not only the bishop, but also the Church itself, as Ryans' name was now connected to the Muldoon case. Of more immediate concern to the bishop, however, was that Ryans was in prison and about to go on trial in open court in Dublin for the crime of child abandonment.

CHAPTER 10

When Ryans was arrested in Keadue in late March 1923 on Mac Eoin's orders, the general maintained that he was charged with three offences relating to anti-Treaty activity. The charges were: illegal possession and use of a revolver in the streets of Mohill, attempting to purchase a machine gun from a sergeant in the National Army garrison in Ballinamore, and the possession of a revolver without proper authority. Mac Eoin claimed that he had intelligence reports and witnesses available to support these very serious charges.[1]

On 18 April 1923, a little over two weeks after his arrest, Fr Ryans was transferred into the custody of the civil authorities at the direction of the adjutant general, the chief administrative officer of the National Army.[2] The transfer was to facilitate his trial for the civil charges relating to the abandonment of baby Rose Brown. Because these charges were due to be heard in early May, it seemed to make sense to proceed initially with them.

Before the transfer took place, Mac Eoin had a meeting with Ryans, while the priest was still in military detention under his command. This meeting would result in a series of correspondence, indicating a remarkable relationship between the high-ranking National Army officer and the imprisoned priest. Given that Ryans and Mac Eoin had known each other from the time they had both spent as political activists in Longford around 1917, it becomes clear that the priest was looking to extract as much benefit as possible from the relationship.

Clearly, Ryans must have had some leverage as, in spite of his role and responsibilities as a commander in the National Army, his acquaintance with Rita Muldoon and his knowledge of what had happened to Paddy, Seán Mac Eoin decided to keep some of Ryans' correspondence, including a statement naming his brother as the child's father, in a private file. They never became part of any investigation into the priest's activities.[3]

The first letter from Fr Ryans to Seán Mac Eoin is undated but was written after their meeting, which appears to have been more of a discussion than an interrogation of a murder suspect.[4] It initially refers to a written statement that Ryans had shown to Mac Eoin at their meeting and which he was now enclosing with his letter. That statement gave his version of events regarding his housekeeper's pregnancy, blaming it on a friend of the Ryans family and describing his own efforts 'to keep it cloaked', which resulted in the Dublin arrest.[5]

The contents of this statement, in its earlier part, were similar to both the response the priest had made to the charging officer, Inspector James O'Gorman, in Dublin, and the defence that he would later put forward in court. But in this version of events given to Mac Eoin, he expanded somewhat by saying that the girl had told him that none of her friends actually knew she was pregnant, but that she was threatening to 'expose the matter'. This led Ryans to believe that he could 'keep it cloaked … if the girl went away for the necessary time'. This plan, and the intention to place the child in care, was upset when they arrived at Dominick Street church in Dublin and found that devotions were in progress. Ryans maintained that the intention was to see the clergy in this church to arrange for the disposal of the child.

While waiting for devotions to conclude, he told of how Mary Kate became impatient and hysterical, and left the child down on a doorstep. From this point, the account given to Mac Eoin differs completely from the sworn statement given to the charging officer, Inspector James O'Gorman. Ryans told Mac Eoin that after placing the child on the doorstep, the young mother had to run to catch up with him, as they had temporarily parted company at that stage. Three witnesses to her action then intervened and, with the help of others, followed and detained her. He himself 'might easily have not waited', but he choose to remain to explain matters to the police when they arrived. This resulted in him being arrested and accused of complicity in the abandonment. Ryans finished by telling Mac Eoin that 'The girl admitted to the police inspector that she alone was responsible and had acted contrary to my orders to her.'

However, the sworn evidence of Inspector James O'Gorman was that the teenage mother had said nothing prior to or after being charged. O'Gorman, while giving his evidence under oath at a preliminary hearing at the City Sessions sitting at Inns Quay Police Court in February 1923, answered some questions put to him. While doing so, he said, 'I read the charge to them and cautioned them. The female deft. [defendant] said nothing.'[6]

Ryans was either being reckless or taking a calculated gamble when he lied to Major General Mac Eoin about events surrounding the abandonment. If Mac Eoin had got an opportunity to read the deposition, he would have seen immediately that Ryans was lying and actually altering his account to cover weaknesses in his own story which had come to light in Inspector O'Gorman's sworn evidence.

If his written statement was reckless, the letter he sent with it was even more extraordinary. It was addressed with the Irish salutation 'A Chara', meaning 'friend'. He began by saying that he had been looking forward to the meeting he had with Mac Eoin and vouched for the correctness of the statement he had previously shown him, which was now enclosed.[7]

Ryans then contradicted the assertion in the enclosed statement that his housekeeper's trouble was caused by an unnamed 'friend of my family' by giving Mac Eoin 'the name that you asked' and proceeding to tell him that it was 'my brother'. The priest was naming his brother Vincent as the father of the child. Ryans would have had Mac Eoin believe that a leading member of the Arigna column had somehow managed a liaison in Aughavas around the time that the National Army was seeking out its members. This information was given on the condition that Mac Eoin not use it in any way except for his 'own private assurance'. This last comment of Fr Ryans suggests that Mac Eoin wanted to be convinced that the priest was innocent of the charge of being the father of Mary Kate's child and above suspicion regarding the murder of Paddy Muldoon.

Ryans went on to ask Mac Eoin straight out to have the proceedings against him in Dublin quashed, and said that he was confident that Mac Eoin had the ability to do so. He again said that he was enclosing the statement he had already shown him, which, he stated, Mac Eoin had agreed would be for himself alone. Then, in a late addition to his letter, Ryans begged Mac Eoin 'for old time & friendship sake to do all you can'.[8]

The priest's next letter to Major General Mac Eoin was headed up 'Dublin' and below that 'Thursday'.[9] Ryans had been handed over to the civil authorities on 18 April 1923, a Wednesday, so he appears to be writing on the following day from Mountjoy Prison. The letter advised that the worst had happened to him as the abandonment case against him had been set for May. He begged Mac Eoin to do anything further he could 'by conversation with the powers that be'.

Ryans was getting desperate. His position had changed from asking Mac Eoin to have the case quashed to doing anything that might help his situation. His letter went on to deny any involvement with the anti-Treaty side, should that be the cause of the government's animosity towards him. This was a blatant lie, of course, as Mac Eoin was well aware of the information that his own intelligence personnel had accumulated concerning Ryans' anti-Treaty activities.

However, the priest felt confident enough of his relationship with Mac Eoin to conclude the letter from Mountjoy with further ambitious requests. He asked Mac Eoin if he could call to visit him. He also requested that Mac Eoin arrange to have his valuable car, which had been impounded by the National Army, returned to the Ryans family home in Keadue. Ryans then, incredulously, suggested that Mac Eoin approach the president on his behalf, as he would surely be able to do something. Finally, as an apparent afterthought, he mentioned that he had asked his family to write to him at Mac Eoin's Athlone military headquarters. Could the major general have any post redirected to him as he was anxious to spare them the pain of knowing he was in jail in Dublin on a civil charge?

The last of these requests – hoping to use Mac Eoin as a postman – suggests a certain brazenness, while also showing that Ryans had somehow kept any knowledge of the civil case from his own family. But as it was now scheduled to take place in open court, its outcome would surely be reported in the papers. This final request appeared on the face of it to be pointless, as his family were bound to become aware of his predicament.

The very next day, 20 April, Major General Mac Eoin wrote back. Addressing Fr Ryans with the Irish salutation 'A Chara', he told him: 'I have done my best, I may be in Dublin Sunday or Monday and will call to see you. I will get your car returned to Keadue and I will forward your letters as directed.'[10]

That same day he instructed the officer commanding, 22nd Battalion, Boyle, County Roscommon, to hand Ryans' car over to his family in Keadue.[11] From this it would seem that the friendship was reciprocated by Mac Eoin.

Mac Eoin, in the midst of the ongoing Civil War, was prepared to make it a priority to see to the requests of a prisoner who had been arrested on a number of serious military charges and was facing trial on a criminal charge, as well as being under investigation for involvement in the murder of a civilian who had been a National Army medical officer. Clearly he was willing to go to surprising lengths to assist his friend. All of this, despite the fact that just ten days earlier he was suggesting, in a report read by Minister for Defence Mulcahy and circulated at the highest levels of government, that Ryans was an accomplice in the murder of Paddy Muldoon. What was his reason for giving Ryans such help and just how far was he prepared to assist him? The two men were clearly more than acquaintances and the level of trust and sharing of intimate details went beyond any sense of loyalty from their War of Independence days.

Whatever other troubles Ryans faced, it is clear that, in

the eyes of the relevant authorities, he was by now firmly implicated in the murder of Paddy Muldoon.

CHAPTER 11

In the early hours of 9 May 1923, the arresting party of Superintendent O'Driscoll and Inspector Mooney from the CID and one of Mac Eoin's officers arrived at the village of Cloone in South Leitrim. This was the village where Fr Ryans produced the automatic revolver and made threats in the company of Rita and Paddy Muldoon in January.

Under cover of darkness the men entered the house of Fr Tom Masterson, a curate of Cloone parish, where they found and detained Mary Kate Gallogly, taking her away well before dawn.[1] The order for her arrest came, it appears, from Minister Kevin O'Higgins.

Mary Kate doesn't appear to have been working as a housekeeper for Fr Masterson and reports of the arrest don't mention whether she was brought to his house by arrangement. Neither was there mention of any search being carried out in the area, so the officers involved seem to have had prior knowledge of where she was that night.

By now Edward Ryans' former housekeeper had not seen her young child since the abandonment in Dublin two months before. The date set for the trial of Mary Kate in Dublin under the name Kate Brown was 9 May. Her co-defendant, Ryans, was already in custody in Mountjoy, awaiting transfer to the courts later that morning. However, there appears to have been no attempt made to bring Mary Kate to Dublin to attend the trial on the charge of abandoning her child. In fact, it would be almost two weeks before Patrick Moynihan, director of the CID, informed the ministry for home affairs that the arrest of Kate Brown had taken place and that the prisoner had been taken to Athlone, the headquarters of Major General Mac Eoin's Western Command.[2]

If the objective of the arrest operation was to prevent Mary Kate Gallogly from attending the court case in Dublin later that day, it was a complete success. Her absence from court meant that only the word of Edward Ryans would be taken as to what had really lain behind the abandonment of the infant. Two substantial witnesses, Mary Kate Gallogly and Paddy Muldoon, were now removed from the process.

***

The court case against Ryans and Mary Kate (under the assumed name of Kate Brown) came before the magistrate, known as the Recorder of Dublin, at the Dublin City Sessions court on Wednesday 9 May. Fr Ryans was indicted for having 'on February 13th 1923, unlawfully abandoned and exposed a child called Rose Brown, she being under two years – namely – two weeks old'.[3] He was also charged with conspiracy to abandon a child.

Full legal teams were present. Mr Carrigan, KC, instructed by the state solicitor, acted for the prosecution, while Fr Ryans was defended by Mr F. Sherry, instructed by Mr Moloney, his solicitor.

Mr Carrigan began proceedings by setting out 'the facts of the case' as gleaned from the sworn statements of witnesses. He stated that on 13 February, the defendant, in company with a young woman, a servant girl, raised the curiosity of a number of residents of inner Dublin in the neighbourhood of Rutland Square when they were seen passing along the streets together. The prosecutor was suggesting here that it was the mismatch between a gentleman and a servant girl that drew the witnesses' attention, possibly the contrast between the thirty-six-year-old man and the frail, poorly dressed young mother half his age.

In contrast, Fr Ryans had told Major General Mac Eoin that the 'girl got impatient and hysterical' after finding the church busy and it was therefore likely that it was her distress that had aroused attention.[4]

Mr Carrigan went on to say that Ryans was carrying a brown paper parcel and his companion was carrying the infant. Three local women, their curiosity aroused, decided on some instinct to follow the couple from street to street until they got as far as St Mary's Church of Ireland, more commonly known as the Black Church, near Broadstone. It was here that the girl laid down the infant on a doorstep across from the church, and then she and the defendant hurried away. The trailing women raised an outcry and the defendant turned back and asked for the child, but the women would not allow him to take it. The police then arrived on the scene and arrested both the prisoner and the young woman.

The prosecutor continued that there was no doubt the child had been deposited as described and that Fr Ryans had put down a paper parcel beside it containing the infant's clothes. The objective was to leave the infant there to be found by some passer-by, with the clothes near it, and taken to some hospital or union. He said that it was regrettable to see the priest in the dock on a charge of this kind, 'but the law could not respect persons, the law was before persons and should be upheld and respected, if a well ordered society was to exist'.[5]

The prosecutor then called as witnesses two of the three women from Lower Dominick Street who had given sworn evidence at the committal hearing: Christina O'Brien and Catherine Ball. The two women repeated the evidence they had given at the committal hearing in February. Mrs O'Brien also said that when Fr Ryans asked her for the child, the gathering crowd told her not to give her to him. Instead she took the infant into Dominick Street vestry, which ironically had been Fr Ryans' original intention.[6] She also confirmed that the parcel contained baby clothes. Mrs Ball corroborated her neighbour's evidence and additionally identified the defendant as the man who had asked for the baby back, to which she had responded, 'Indeed you won't get the baby.'

The next witness, Constable Murphy, stated that when he arrived the crowd had the prisoner and the woman 'held up'. Inspector James O'Gorman then gave evidence stating that he was in the Bridewell station when the defendant and the girl were brought in, and confirmed that he had charged Fr Ryans with abandoning the baby. He went on to repeat the evidence he had given to the committal hearing in February and said that Ryans had stated that the father of the child was a worthless fellow, who could not provide a home for anyone and marriage was out of the question. The priest also said that the father was a friend of his family and that is why he, Ryans, took an interest in the case. He added that Ryans provided lodging and paid expenses for three months for the girl in Dublin and that at the time they were on their way to see the clergy in Dominick Street to arrange for the 'disposal' of the child.[7]

With the case for the prosecution closed, Fr Ryans took the witness box and said that he wished to make the same statement as he did to the inspector when initially charged.[8] He then expanded on why he took an interest in the case, saying that the girl was employed temporarily by him as a housekeeper and she accused an individual who used to visit him in his house of being responsible for her condition. That individual was a friend of his family and 'naturally he was anxious to have the matter cloaked up'.

At this stage he was contradicting his earlier written statement to Major General Mac Eoin, in which he had said that his own brother, Vincent, was the father of the child. Ryans then repeated his earlier contention that the father was a worthless individual, which left him with no alternative but to make provision for 'the girl' to go away for a while. He claimed she had sent word to him after the baby was born and that he came to Dublin to carry out the rest of the plan he had conceived.

Fr Ryans completed his testimony by saying that he could have simply walked away from the curious locals if he had wished, but he stayed because he thought he could explain the matter. This suggestion of his, that he had nothing to hide and was merely giving assistance to his housekeeper, could be safely made, as his co-defendant was not in court to testify otherwise.

With all the witnesses heard, the prosecutor and counsel for the defence made their closing arguments to the jury. The recorder, in charging the jury, said that every citizen of Dublin should be proud of the action of the local women in following the couple and protecting the two-week-old infant from exposure. In saying this, the recorder would have been conscious that the incident took place between 7 and 8 p.m. on a wet mid-February night.

The jury returned after only an hour's absence, with the foreman stating that it was impossible for them to come to an agreement. His Honour, the recorder, could not give them any assistance and therefore the prisoner was put back for a retrial.

Up to this point the charges against Fr Ryans had been the focus of the court case; there had not been any discussion of the failure of his co-defendant to appear. Normally, when a defendant fails to make an appearance, in the absence of an acceptable explanation, a warrant might be issued by the presiding judge for his or her arrest. In this case, none was issued. The newspaper report makes no mention of whether Mary Kate was legally represented on the day.

The prosecution then indicated to the court that it was entering a 'nolle prosequi' in the case of Mary Kate (under the name Kate Brown); that is to say that they did not intend pursuing her prosecution at this stage.[9] This decision by the prosecution to drop the case against her is not explained in the newspaper report, suggesting no explanation was given to the court. Still, the prosecution made it clear that they intended to pursue a second trial against her co-accused, Fr Ryans, in spite of the evidence against him being almost identical to the evidence against Mary Kate. In what was a highly unusual move, Fr Ryans was remanded in jail until the retrial.

***

Sometime after her arrest in the dead of night, a very troubled and vulnerable Mary Kate Gallogly arrived at the Ladies Detention Camp in Athlone Castle.[10] She was placed in a cell already occupied by three female republican activists.[11] They immediately questioned her to eliminate the possibility that she was there to spy on them.

Initially, Mary Kate lied to them, maintaining that she was a dispatch rider, or message carrier, for John Charlie

Keegan of Leitrim, the same man previously identified by Mac Eoin as the leader of the gang that shot Dr Muldoon. Mary Kate may have been aware of his notoriety as he lived only three miles from her parents' home, or she may have come across him as one of Fr Ryans' anti-Treaty contacts. However, a few careful questions from her cellmates proved to them that her claimed association with Keegan was false. This left them wondering if she had indeed been introduced into their company to spy on them. Even after her lies were exposed, she didn't tell them the truth; perhaps she thought it better to be considered a potential spy than the abandoner of her own baby who had been born out of wedlock.

After only a few days in captivity, two of Mary Kate's cellmates were transferred to Mountjoy Prison in Dublin. The woman left behind then discovered Mary Kate's secret. Elizabeth 'Baby' Bohan was a long-standing Cumann na mBan member from Ballymote in County Sligo who had taken the anti-Treaty side. She had been imprisoned by the National Army since the previous month. In a letter she wrote to her married sister, Oonagh Brady, on 17 May 1923, Baby Bohan revealed that 'a little girl about 18 or 19 years old' was imprisoned with her and that since being left alone together she had discovered the sad truth. Although Baby had very strong Catholic views, they were tempered by a genuine Christian spirit. This allowed her take a more kindly view of someone who would have been regarded, at that time, as a fallen woman. Baby developed a protective attitude towards her young cellmate: 'the child who is here, could hardly be called a woman and she is most nervous – I often wonder at what'.[12]

This caring generosity towards Kate was not confined to their daily contact. Often, Baby would lie awake at night, listening, as Kate 'could not sleep at all without the gas being lit and then she talks all night through, poor girl'.[13]

Mary Kate Gallogly was clearly deeply affected by all that she had gone through: the pregnancy, birth and painful separation from her daughter. She would also have been aware of the rumours circulating in her community connecting her pregnancy to Fr Ryans and, in turn, to Dr Muldoon's murder. Baby Bohan provides us with an extremely sympathetic and clear description of Mary Kate, her youth and her vulnerability.

What Mary Kate couldn't have known then was that, by the time she was imprisoned with Baby Bohan, her infant daughter Rose had already died. After her abandonment in Dublin city, Rose had been taken to Pelletstown, an institution known later as Saint Patrick's Mother and Baby Home. It was originally a public workhouse but had been designated a 'special institution' exclusively for single mothers in 1904. It was run on behalf of the civil authorities by the Sisters of the Daughters of Saint Vincent de Paul (later called the Daughters of Charity). The institution was also used as a 'holding centre' for unaccompanied babies and children until their transfer to orphanages or homes. Having been separated from her mother, Mary Kate's infant survived for just a month and a half in care.[14]

While Mary Kate was spared the rigours of a trial on the abandonment charge, her personal situation would not get any better in the immediate future. Her only source of comfort in Athlone, Baby Bohan, was transferred some time later to Kilmainham Jail in Dublin, which left Mary Kate alone again.

***

The trial of Edward Ryans for abandonment was reported in only one newspaper, *The Irish Times*. None of the other national papers carried reports of what must have been an unusual case, given the drama of the capture and arrest of this Catholic priest and his housekeeper.

The local papers also ignored the proceedings. Neither the *Leitrim Observer* nor *The Leitrim Advertiser* carried any report. However, the *Leitrim Observer*'s first edition after the hearing did report on the national appeal organised for the benefit of Rita Muldoon and her young family by Paddy's former colleagues, Dr Reynolds and Dr Dolan, with Canon Masterson as treasurer, which raised in the region of £500. At the top of the long list of donators published in the *Leitrim Observer* on 12 May 1923 was the Most Rev. Dr Hoare, Bishop of Ardagh and Clonmacnois. Medical colleagues from throughout Ireland and some from abroad were heavily represented among the list of the many who donated.

Members of the clergy were also noticeably represented, but in slightly lesser numbers. Fr Edward Ryans, Paddy Muldoon's one-time acquaintance, does not appear on the published list of donors.

When forwarding a donation of £10, the bishop had sent an accompanying letter to the organisers of the fund, which was also published in the *Observer* that day. In it he wrote:

> The foul murder of Dr Muldoon inflicts a stain upon the good name of Mohill town and parish and upon the entire diocese. The only means left to us of expiating this awful deed is to pray for the deceased, to help those for whom he laboured, and to beseech God to bring the heartless assassin to penance.

It would seem that two months after the murder, the impact of the event on the reputation of the diocese was a major concern to the bishop. He advised his flock to subscribe to the collection and to hope for penitence from the perpetrator, as opposed to justice for Dr Muldoon's family. Rising to his religious theme the bishop went on to say:

> Oh! How the worm of remorse must gnaw at the murderer's heart and mind and drive him out a hated fugitive on this earth – the earth which still, thank God, shudders at the sin of Cain, the first on the list that cries to heaven for vengeance.

In the Old Testament the Lord marked out Cain to be forever

a fugitive and wanderer on earth as a penance for the murder of his brother, Abel.

By this stage Bishop Hoare would have known about the rumours linking Fr Ryans to the murder of Paddy Muldoon. The gossip circulating among his diocesan clergy and laity alike would have been reported to him. The bishop had already expelled Ryans from his Aughavas curacy and residence; this letter appears to be indicating that amends for the foul murder of Paddy Muldoon could suitably be made by penitence and exile alone. While Bishop Hoare couldn't be expected to lead the criminal investigation, his letter, obviously written for publication, contained no appeal to the community to assist the police in apprehending the culprits.

The Freeman's Journal, a national paper, also managed to find space for Bishop Hoare's letter, but it too somehow failed to report on Ryans' abandonment trial.[15]

It remained to be seen if the bishop's token remedy of penitence and exile would be deemed sufficient reparation for the brutal murder of an innocent man and an ever-increasing amount of collateral damage.

***

Shortly after the inconclusive trial, Edward Ryans wrote again to Major General Mac Eoin from Mountjoy Prison.[16] Ryans felt that the charges against him could now be easily and quickly quashed. He suggested that damage had already been done to his reputation by the publicity surrounding the case. He went on to mention the outstanding military charges against him and the hope that these would be quickly dealt with after he was passed back into military custody. Ryans thanked Mac Eoin for a letter he had recently sent him, enclosing a cheque he was forwarding on behalf of another party.

Some days later, on 21 May, Mac Eoin wrote to a priest, a Fr Meehan, attaching a copy of Edward Ryans' letter acknowledging receipt of the cheque. Fr Terence Meehan had been a curate in Keadue from 1917 to 1918 where the Ryans family lived, and is likely to have known Fr Ryans through that connection. Like Ryans, he had also acted as a judge in the Sinn Féin courts. The cheque might have represented money from Ryans' personal funds, or could have come from another source, such as a priests' benevolent society or the republican movement.

A copy of Mac Eoin's covering letter to Fr Meehan is marked for the major general's private file, the one maintained for certain documents relating to Fr Ryans.[17] It is not clear why Mac Eoin would provide a copy of Ryans' entire letter if Fr Meehan's only interest was safe delivery of the cheque. What is clear, however, was that at least one member of the clergy would seem to have been using Mac Eoin as a conduit to Fr Ryans.

On 24 May 1923, an order was issued by Frank Aiken, chief of staff of the IRA, to cease fire and dump arms. Nine weeks after Paddy Muldoon was murdered on the fringes of the Civil War, the conflict had come to an end. A process was started to deal with the anti-Treaty republicans. It involved detaining thousands of them in the summer of 1923 to prevent a return to hostilities.

Two days after the May ceasefire announcement, Fr Ryans, still imprisoned in Mountjoy, wrote his final letter to Bishop Hoare, or at least the last one to have survived.[18] It was a little over two weeks since his initial trial and Ryans could probably see that the ending of hostilities had changed the political landscape and might be of benefit to his situation. In any event, in the immediate aftermath of the end of hostilities, he felt in a position to reopen his old struggle with his bishop.

Yet again the letter is almost totally given over to a militant defence of his situation and an almost paranoid attitude towards those he sees as opposing or denigrating him. In the final paragraph, Ryans denies emphatically that he was in league with, or gave assistance to, either the armed or un-armed anti-Treaty opposition. While this would be shown to be untrue by his own later admissions, at least it was clear what he was denying.

However, the subject of another denial in the letter was not as clear. Ryans had commenced by referring to a copy of a letter the bishop had sent him in July the previous year. Ryans maintained that 'the particulars it contained were false', but he was unable to deal effectively with it at the time as he was not told either who the letter writer was or who was a party to it. This letter, he felt, may have influenced the bishop's attitude towards him.

While the mystery letter may have accused him of anti-Treaty activity, it might as easily have related to his housekeeper's situation. Assuming that Mary Kate Gallogly's pregnancy went to full term, she would have been about three months pregnant in July 1922, the month the letter was sent to the bishop.

If Dr Muldoon had told his friend Canon Masterson of Fr Ryans' problem, there is a strong likelihood that the canon would have informed Bishop Hoare. This might explain the letter that was sent to the bishop in July 1922 and was still troubling Ryans, as he faced a second trial on the child abandonment charges a year later.

It might also account for the meeting in Fr Deniston's residence in Cloone in January 1923 and Ryans' behaviour that night. That meeting apparently had been arranged, or utilised, by Paddy and Rita Muldoon to canvass support among his fellow clergy for Fr Ryans to do the right thing in dealing with Mary Kate's pregnancy. Whatever about the noble intentions behind the meeting, it ultimately proved to be a catalyst for tragedy.

In this final letter to the bishop, Fr Ryans is unable to resist a rebuke to his superior, claiming that his present situation, imprisonment in Mountjoy, is 'with your Lordship's consent'.[19] This is either a taunt at the bishop for not using his influence to obtain his release, or an accusation that Ryans' continued imprisonment was sanctioned by the bishop and suited his purposes.

Fr Ryans goes on to mention the 'horrors and indignities' of his present position and his name being 'wrongfully dragged through the mire by uncharitable clergy and laity'. He maintains that 'all the prejudice of the Civil Authorities will be of no avail' and that the military authorities' great show in arresting him was based on charges that 'were only a sham'. He then refers directly to collusion when he says that he was aware 'there was a great deal of consultation and connivance as to how to deal most effectively with me'.

At this point the actual level of consultation and connivance in the Ryans case was not yet clear. Furthermore, there is no record of a direct response by Bishop Hoare to Fr Ryans' letter.

CHAPTER 12

On Sunday 27 May 1923, just over two months after Paddy Muldoon's death, the affair seems to have claimed another casualty. Fr Edward Dunne, the young priest who Rita Muldoon had confronted regarding an alleged breach of confidence two months earlier, died in tragic circumstances at thirty-two years of age. The cause of death was certified as 'delirium tremens – 2 days, heart failure – two hours'. The young curate had apparently died in the aftermath of a period of sustained alcohol abuse.[1] But what exactly had driven the priest to the point where he drank himself into an early grave?

Interestingly, not everybody mourned his passing. The day after his death a letter made its way through the postal system that cast more light on the role of Fr Dunne in what had come to pass. This letter was sent by Margaret Ellis, or Maggie as she was known, who was related to the Muldoons and had been one of the chief mourners at Paddy Muldoon's funeral.[2] She wrote to Rita's brother Ambrose, enclosing a copy of Paddy's death certificate, which she had obtained from Dr Redahan at his request.[3]

In her letter she referred Ambrose to that day's newspaper, which carried news of Fr Dunne's death, saying that 'this is the scoundrel that got poor Dear P murdered to save his own skin[,] poor Paddy was innocent T.G. [Thank God] even of having the slightest thing to do with Ryans['] suspension'.

The clear inference is that it was Fr Dunne, and not Paddy Muldoon, either directly or through Canon Masterson, who had informed Bishop Hoare of the full details of Edward Ryans' situation, which had led to Ryans' suspension, and that Dunne had then somehow convinced Ryans that it was Paddy or Rita Muldoon who had told the bishop. This would account for Fr Ryans' fury towards Rita after Mr Duignan from Fenagh met him at Dromod railway station and told him about the contents of the letter addressed to Rita, information that Rita felt indicated a possible breach of confidence by Fr Dunne. Rita had no doubt that Fr Ryans had been informed of all that she had discussed with Fr Dunne when she confronted him about the breach of confidence.

Maggie Ellis, although a religious woman, was showing no sympathy for a young local priest who had died the previous day. Instead she claimed that the priest's self-interest and deceit had helped result in the death of Paddy Muldoon. Furthermore, she feared that if the general public came to feel that Paddy Muldoon was the cause of Ryans' suspension from his parish, members of the clergy would use that against Rita and her children sometime in the future. Maggie told Ambrose that she expected him to make both Bishop Hoare and Canon Masterson have Paddy Muldoon's innocence declared in the public press.

Edward Dunne's involvement in the motives behind Paddy Muldoon's murder – whether by passing the blame for Ryans' suspension onto Paddy, or simply by betraying Rita's confidence and going to Ryans with information that would likely have stoked Ryans' volatile temper – would certainly explain the mental anguish he was under in the weeks before his death. The young priest, whose character had been questioned by Rita Muldoon, must have been shocked by Paddy's murder. He must also have been aware that he was being associated with its cause by some people in the locality. The guilt he felt would undoubtedly have lain heavily on his mind, and may well have simply been too much for him to endure.

Whatever the reasons, he was the second of the attendees at the fateful January meeting in Fr Deniston's Cloone residence to die in tragic circumstances. And one thing is for certain – Bishop Hoare was now facing a scandal in his diocese of proportions never previously experienced in his long episcopate.

Meanwhile, Maggie Ellis' insights into the motives behind her cousin Paddy's murder were not restricted to what she had written in her letter to Ambrose Lee. As well as being a shopkeeper, Maggie had worked voluntarily alongside Rita Muldoon in the Mohill District Nursing Association,[4] the ladies association involved in child welfare and helping the sick, weak and helpless of the district.[5] The women of this association made home visits to look after the sick and needy.

They also employed a full-time nurse to assist with more specialised visits relating to midwifery, medical and surgical needs.

Sometime during 1922, Rita and Maggie would have become aware, through their work with the association, of the pregnancy of Mary Kate Gallogly. While Maggie would likely have been cautious in her approach to what was viewed as an extremely delicate subject, Rita was more inclined to discuss the need for provision to be made for the young mother, and even for support to be provided to assist Fr Ryans – whom she felt to be the father of the child – to shoulder his responsibilities. Many years later, Maggie voiced the belief that Rita's principled, though probably naïve, approach may well have contributed to Edward Ryans' later murderous reaction.[6]

***

In the aftermath of the Civil War, the nascent Free State had to deal with the legacy of compensation claims for deaths, injuries, damage to infrastructure and property, and theft, which occurred during the Civil War and the earlier conflict. Like many others who had suffered loss, Rita Muldoon was now starting to come to some sort of terms with her grief and was trying to get on with her life. Although broken-hearted, she wouldn't have wanted her young children to see her perpetually tearful, as that would only add to their insecurity following the death of their father. They were now more dependent on her than ever, and she had another child on the way to consider. So she set about securing a financial future for herself and her family as best she could.

A month after her husband's death, Rita had been granted administration of Paddy's estate, which was valued at £2,050.[7] The grant of administration came through two weeks after the advertised sale of valuable items by public auction on behalf of the representatives of the late Dr M. P. Muldoon. In early October Rita received a cheque for a further £20 10s 6d, a final payment for the services Paddy gave to National Army soldiers. It was a poignant reminder of the loss of the family's sole earner, someone who had devoted his working life to the health and well-being of others. She also had the £500 raised by the special appeal.

However, none of this would be enough to keep her going indefinitely and so an appeal to the State for compensation was her next logical step. Rita was fortunate to have her brother Ambrose to assist her through the compensation process, at what was a very difficult time for her. Following advice and directions received from Minister for Agriculture Patrick Hogan, in April 1923 Ambrose arranged for John A. Pettit of Carrick-on-Shannon, the solicitor acting on behalf of the Muldoon family compensation claim, to submit a claim for £20,000.[8]

On 22 July 1923, Rita Muldoon gave birth to a baby boy in Dublin, just over four months after her husband's murder. The boy was christened Patrick Michael, in memory of his father. By all accounts it was a difficult birth and it must have been extremely emotional for Rita as well.

Soon after this, she was once again attempting to bring in money to support her family. While she was recuperating in Denmark House, a Dublin nursing home in Lower Leeson Street, she used the opportunity to write to Hannan & O'Brien, a firm of solicitors in Longford, about a debt of £30 that was owed to Paddy by a garage owner, a Mr Adair. Hannan & O'Brien responded on 31 July to say that they would do their best to recover the debt.[9]

At least housing was not a concern. By this time, Rita had moved back to live in Clifden. Fortunately, her father, a successful businessman, had built a terrace of four houses, Lees Terrace (now known as Riverside), with one house for each of his four daughters. It was a modest dwelling by comparison to Coolebawn House, where the family had lived in Mohill, with two or three bedrooms, a living room and kitchen. It didn't have a large back garden, but the children had the freedom of the local countryside and beaches to roam.[10]

Once she'd returned from Dublin, Rita got on with looking after her young family, a demanding task for a widow and single parent. Remarkably, she began working as a rate collector sometime that year, most likely on a part-time basis.[11] It is likely that she started in this career alongside her brother, who was also a rate collector.

This was undoubtedly a dangerous occupation at the time. The non-payment of rates for political reasons during the

War of Independence had continued during the Civil War; in some instances for reasons of principle, while others hedged their bets awaiting the outcome of the hostilities. This left considerable cases of rate arrears to be followed up after the end of the war, and it was common for rate collectors to be accompanied by Civic Guards when embarking on some of their more difficult cases. It was certainly not an occupation for the faint-hearted in the early years of the Free State, but Rita Muldoon had the courage, as well as the financial need, to take on the position.

Rita had begun 1923 as a happily married Leitrim doctor's wife, but had finished the year a widow, devastated by her husband's murder, having to augment her income with a sometimes dangerous occupation in Galway. She was also awaiting the outcome of her compensation claim and was desperate to see progress being made in obtaining justice for the murder of her husband.

CHAPTER 13

The Rev. Edward Ryans came up for trial for the second time before the recorder at Green Street courthouse, Dublin, on 12 July 1923.[1] Again the case against him was prosecuted by Mr Carrigan, but on this occasion, Ryans, the former Sinn Féin judge, acted in his own defence. That decision may have arisen from the lack of diocesan financial support for the priest, or possibly disagreement over any conditions that might have been attached to such support.

In setting out the case for the prosecution, Mr Carrigan began by passing on some news of what had happened to Mary Kate Gallogly. He informed the court that she was now in a lunatic asylum. No other details were given in court, but this was six weeks after Mary Kate had been detained in military custody in Athlone alongside Baby Bohan.

The news that the woman he had put through the ordeal of child abandonment was now in such distress did not seem to give Fr Ryans pause. Nor did it deter him from cross-examining the witnesses who were called again to give evidence. He was prone to arguing directly with Crown Prosecutor Carrigan and he even addressed the jury directly.[2] After hearing the evidence, and following about half an hour's deliberation, the jury again failed to reach a unanimous decision and the recorder discharged them.

The recorder then suggested personal bail for the defendant, but the crown prosecutor objected. Apparently Ryans had already applied for bail in advance of the second trial, but the prosecutor now disclosed that the attorney general would not allow bail under any circumstances or for any amount of money. The recorder at Green Street considered the refusal to allow bail in these circumstances to be somewhat harsh. He suggested to Fr Ryans that he could pursue the matter before a higher court, the King's Bench, where he felt bail would surely be granted.

At this stage Ryans had been held in detention for over three months, and the recorder would have been conscious that the typical sentence for being found guilty of child abandonment in that period was usually about one month's imprisonment.[3] However, the authorities seemed intent on treating Ryans as a special case and keeping him in prison. In spite of having dismissed the charges against his co-accused, Mary Kate Gallogly, the prosecutors were intent on pursuing the case for a third time against Fr Ryans. It was clear that they, and others, wanted Ryans to be kept locked up and out of circulation.[4]

The legal authorities were not the only ones who wanted to keep a close eye on Ryans. Just a week after the second trial, the Catholic chaplain to Mountjoy Prison, Fr M. S. McMahon, reported back to Bishop Hoare to say that the bishop's 'kind intervention did not prove as effective as was hoped'.[5] Clearly the bishop was paying close attention to

Ryans' case, though McMahon doesn't record the nature of his intervention.

The chaplain also mentioned the outcome of the second trial, discussing Ryans' performance in his own defence before a full court. After a detailed account of Ryans' efforts to obtain bail, the chaplain turned his attention to the forthcoming third trial. He felt that 'if the jury acquits him the scandal will in great part be repaired', but his own expectation was that there would be yet another inconclusive outcome and that Ryans would hardly be tried for a fourth time.

Fr McMahon had a very good understanding of the legal system. With his experience, excellent contacts and access to the prison, he was ideally placed to monitor Ryans' situation on the bishop's behalf. He further advised Bishop Hoare that, in the event of the civil charges being dropped, the military authorities might keep Ryans in custody and prosecute him on 'one of the many alleged charges against him'. Then the chaplain, presumably referring back to the earlier failed intervention by Bishop Hoare, told him, 'It is hard to see what more your Lordship can do in the circumstances.'

Fr McMahon finished his report by promising to keep the bishop informed 'if there should be any move made'. In looking to the future, the chaplain said that they 'must only await events & hope that scandal may be removed or atoned for'. Notably the focus is on atonement and controlling the scandal, rather than having justice done.

The letter also omits any reference to the crown prosecutor's announcement that Mary Kate was now in a mental asylum. Both Bishop Hoare and Fr McMahon were likely already aware of her committal.

***

Bishop Hoare and another of the men looking in on this case from the sidelines, Seán Mac Eoin, had dealings with one another prior to the Muldoon incident. Following the bishop's denunciation of the republican movement in the aftermath of the killing of an RIC constable in Ballinalee on 1 November 1920, during the War of Independence, Commandant Mac Eoin went to his residence in Longford town to argue the IRA's case.

After being received by the bishop, Mac Eoin proceeded to explain that he was a properly appointed officer of the Irish Republican Army, serving a lawful government through its minister for defence and headquarters staff. Furthermore, that government had been voted into office by the elected parliament of the Irish people. He maintained that the IRA was fighting a defensive battle, adhering to customary methods of warfare, and that they took life only in self-defence and in defence of the nation and its parliament.

Mac Eoin also pointed out how the Irish bishops had already declared that Ireland was entitled to its freedom. Bishop Hoare himself had accepted Sinn Féin's landslide victory in the 1918 general election as the people's decision on the future of Ireland. In his Lenten pastoral of 1919 he had stated that 'Ireland demands to be a free and independent Nation, and all Nations, except England, acknowledge the justice of our claim.'[6]

Bishop Hoare, like many people in Ireland at the time, was challenged by the reality of republican violence. However, he accepted Mac Eoin's arguments, telling him that his words of condemnation did not apply now that he could see that the IRA was a properly constituted body. The young commandant came away from the meeting with his bishop's blessing and the belief that he had forged an understanding and struck up a friendship.

A few months after the murder of Dr Muldoon, the two men again came together, this time to rectify an unfortunate incident. The circumstances of this event provide some evidence of how the relationship between the general and the bishop had developed since their initial meeting.

On Sunday 22 July 1923, a unit of Free State soldiers attending a public Mass in Carrick-on-Shannon was shocked when the priest, Fr Dalton, denounced the army from the altar as 'cowards, obscene and filthy tongued blackguards, drunkards, and as the corrupters of the youth of the country'.[7] He then went further and advised the mixed congregation that, 'as they were the paymasters they should get rid of those scoundrels immediately'.

There is evidence to suggest the outburst may have been connected to above-normal levels of venereal disease in garrison towns at the time.[8] However, the soldiers present were incensed and later that morning informed their superior officers that they would not attend Mass again until the priest's statements were either proven or withdrawn.

The next day two officers of the Carrick-on-Shannon command, Captains Seamus Baxter and George Geraghty, wrote to Bishop Hoare to make known to him the grievance of their men at Fr Dalton's sermon.[9] The two officers added their own support to the men's complaint and respectfully requested the bishop to call on Fr Dalton to publicly prove the truth of his statements, or else to withdraw and apologise publicly for them.

While their men's grievance was understandable, Captains Baxter and Geraghty exhibited a certain moral courage in relaying this complaint in the manner they did. It wouldn't necessarily benefit a man's career prospects in the army to raise a contentious issue with a member of the Catholic hierarchy. As it transpired, their commanding officer did not support their stance.

Major General Mac Eoin considered the action taken by his two officers as 'entirely arbitrary and a grave violation [of] the Military discipline concerning such matters'.[10] He believed that the two officers had gone entirely outside their authority in reporting the complaint to the bishop, instead of going through the higher ranks of the army. Mac Eoin set out this belief in a letter to Bishop Hoare a week later, and added that he sincerely regretted 'the annoyance caused your Lordship by the report in question'.[11] He also said that, assuming Fr Dalton did make the statements attributed to him, he did not think the priest would be able to substantiate them.

In any event, as Dalton was not a military chaplain, Mac Eoin's view was that the issue was one for the bishop to deal with, which is what Baxter and Geraghty had requested the bishop do in their letter to him. Mac Eoin also informed Bishop Hoare that 'in view of the highly nervous state of the body politic at the moment it would be more prudent to reprimand the troops paraded for that purpose within the confines of their own barracks. All embarrassment would be saved in this way.'

Mac Eoin's subservient apology to the bishop remarkably ended with his intention of reprimanding his aggrieved troops. He was quite willing to leave the question of censure of Fr Dalton to the bishop; he had no intention of interfering and didn't request to be advised on the outcome of Bishop Hoare's investigations.

The bishop wrote back, thanking Mac Eoin for his 'amicable letter' and told him that he had not investigated the case but had responded in writing to Baxter and Geraghty.[12] He had informed the two officers 'that to allude to the matter from the Pulpit again would only give greater publicity to the charge of Fr Dalton and would therefore do more harm than good'. In conclusion, the bishop told Mac Eoin that he would deal with the case 'and I think anything further would mar what we all stand for'.[13]

It seems obvious from this episode that both Mac Eoin and Bishop Hoare were of the belief that justice did not need to be seen to be done when the shared interests of Church and State were in play. They were both more interested in procedures and public perception than in the veracity of the complaint. Therefore, it is abundantly clear that they were quite capable of drawing a cloak over other unpalatable matters that might embarrass their organisations and, in fact, would readily combine to do so.

***

The third trial of Fr Edward Ryans on the child abandonment charges came before Mr Justice Pim on 10 August 1923.[14] Ryans again conducted his own defence, claiming that the prosecution was pressing the case excessively against him and complaining of being kept in custody. He characterised the evidence being given against him as reckless and unreliable.

During the course of the trial, it was disclosed (the newspaper report does not indicate by whom) that Mary Kate Gallogly was still in an asylum. The court was also given the information that baby Rose was now dead. The death of the infant, whose welfare had ostensibly formed the basis for the charges against Fr Ryans, appears to have been given only a brief mention, without any detail.

A search of death records from Rose Brown's known birth on 29 January 1923 to the date of the third trial produced only one applicable record. It relates to the death from gastritis of a female infant, age given as three months, at Pelletstown, Castleknock, County Dublin on 31 March 1923.[15] It appears Rose was already dead by the time the case of her abandonment came to court for three separate trials during the summer of 1923.

The news of her death made no discernible impact on the case. Fr McMahon, the prison chaplain, was proved correct: the jury again failed to reach an agreement and Ryans was again remanded in custody.

Remarkably, once again the only newspaper to carry a report of Fr Ryans' trial was *The Irish Times*, the Protestant and former unionist paper. The other national and provincial newspapers provided no details of any of the three trials. And it wasn't that cases involving clergy were not reported. For example, on the day of the first trial, 9 May, both *The Freeman's Journal* and the *Irish Independent* carried a detailed account of a court case relating to a motor accident where the Reverend William Harvey, from the Church of Ireland on the Sandford Road, Ranelagh, Dublin, had been knocked off his motorbike and badly injured by a car driven by a Mr Cronhelm, who had been drinking.[16] The following day, when both papers should have been carrying details of Fr Ryans' trial, they found space to update their readership on the outcome of Rev. Harvey's case: he was awarded £1,187, plus costs.[17]

Moreover, in the days after the first trial, the national *Freeman's Journal* and local *Leitrim Observer* referred to Bishop Hoare's 'sin of Cain' letter, yet left out any mention of the trial itself.[18] It would appear that, apart from *The Irish Times*, the Irish national and provincial papers bowed to pressure and censored their own publications. The only body that gained from this self-imposed censorship, of course, was the Catholic Church.

Effectively, this meant that about eighty per cent of the reading public of the national dailies, and a higher percentage of Catholics, did not have access to a newspaper report on the abandonment case. The success of this newspaper censorship can be gauged by the fact that the public, particularly many in the local Leitrim community, were unaware of what happened to baby Rose for many years.

CHAPTER 14

While Fr Edward Ryans spent most of 1923 in prison, fighting the child abandonment charge, the other man named in relation to the murder of Paddy Muldoon remained at large.

John Charles Keegan, the man referred to by Major General Mac Eoin and CID Director Patrick Moynihan as the prime suspect for Dr Muldoon's murder, was not an imposing figure. He was five foot eight inches tall, with dark-brown hair and blue eyes, and weighed 155 pounds.[1] Keegan was battle hardened from his time as a Volunteer fighting against the crown forces during the War of Independence, and from his subsequent time on the run from the National Army after escaping his death sentence. He was also a notoriously difficult man to catch.

Charlie Eddie McGoohan, a comrade of Keegan's during the War of Independence and a member of the National Army, was incensed at Keegan's conversion to the anti-Treaty cause. McGoohan had risked his own life to capture some of the prisoners Keegan had helped escape from Longford Barracks and he set out on a personal mission to recapture Keegan. McGoohan even dressed as an anti-Treaty fighter himself on occasion as he travelled the South Leitrim area looking for Keegan.

One day, as McGoohan was driving on his own in an old Ford Model T on a road near Cloone, he spotted Keegan coming towards him on a jaunting car.[2] McGoohan immediately stopped his car as Keegan, simultaneously recognising him, jumped from the jaunting car and ran into the fields. McGoohan grabbed his revolver and gave chase for about 200 yards, while firing off ten shots at Keegan at a distance of about twenty yards.

McGoohan had earned a certain reputation as a marksman. He had shot dead Constable Wilfred Jones, a Black and Tan, in a close-quarters gunfight in Ballinamore in April 1921. However, it was Keegan's reputation as elusive and athletic that held up during their encounter in Cloone that day, as he made good his escape through the hedgerows. McGoohan's belief was 'that I drilled some holes in his clothing but he got clean away'.

John Charles Keegan had escaped death for the second time.

Shortly after escaping execution, Keegan was involved in the attack on Paddy Muldoon that resulted in the young doctor's death. However, Rita Muldoon was firmly of the belief that her husband's three attackers were deceived into carrying out the killing, and she herself was more concerned in pursuing the man she believed to be the real instigator of the crime, Fr Ryans.[3]

The fact that someone who had just broken out of jail to escape his own execution could, within a matter of days, shoot dead an unarmed civilian showed a chilling lack of empathy, even if there was an element of deception involved. Such behaviour was all the more abnormal when we learn that, on his own admission, John Charles Keegan had previously been treated for bronchitis by Paddy Muldoon, so his victim was known to him.[4]

Keegan was clearly an unstable individual. Commandant Luke Smyth of the 23rd Infantry Battalion left little room for doubt in a description he gave of Keegan in a report to his GOC, Major General Mac Eoin. He referred to Keegan as the only dangerous man in the battalion area and said, 'My opinion of him is that he is not right in his mind.'[5] Smyth was probably describing a person to whom we would more commonly refer today as a psychopath. His subsequent actions during this turbulent period would further underline this description.

***

On Monday night, 19 March, the day after Paddy Muldoon's death, an off-duty National Army soldier, Edward Fitzgerald, was shot dead in Ballinamuck, about eight miles south of Mohill, just over the border in County Longford. He had been sitting beside the fire in the kitchen of Duignan's public house (known today as The 98 Bar).

Fitzgerald was from Mohill and three of his brothers had served with the British Army in the First World War. All three had been killed. Fitzgerald himself had been a porter with the Hibernian Bank prior to enlisting in the National Army, and he was his widowed mother's only source of income.[6] Although still in uniform, he was unarmed when the back door of the pub burst open and several shots were fired at him by one attacker, who had the support of other armed men outside.

The badly injured soldier died while he was being driven to hospital in Longford town by a local priest, Fr Cosgrove.[7] In one of his series of IRA pension applications, John Charles Keegan wrote with reference to his Civil War activities: 'I went to Ballinamuck an Shot one Soldier an told 2 Soldiers in a Bar one of you dies tomorrow [*sic*]'.[8]

When Edward Fitzgerald was shot, there was at least one other National Army soldier in Duignan's pub, who had been sent to bring Fitzgerald back to the local barracks. This would tally with Keegan's account. In any case, Fitzgerald's sister and his nephew were always of the belief that Keegan shot him. This belief was based on local knowledge, including reports that Keegan and his gang were seen out that night in the area.[9] Keegan's own pension application also seems to confirm that he was indeed the assailant that night.

***

Three days after the death of Edward Fitzgerald, Sunday Mass-goers arriving at several South Leitrim Catholic churches found very alarming notices displayed nearby. The handwritten notices were signed 'O.C., 3rd Battalion, 3rd

South Leitrim Brigade, Irish Republican Army'. Firstly, they stated that 'if any soldier of the Third Battalion Area, now in military custody, be executed, all doctors, priests and ministers, natives of Longford County will have to clear out of the above-mentioned area, twenty-four hours after the executions'.[10]

Keegan's older brother, Michael Joe Keegan, who was also active on the anti-Treaty side, had been captured by the National Army that week, and other prominent local anti-Treaty soldiers had also recently been rounded up.[11] The reference to Longford natives possibly related to the fact that executions ordered by the Free State authorities had been carried out under the command of Major General Mac Eoin.

The notices went on to say that any person assisting 'the Free State or giving information which might lead to the capture of a soldier of the IRA will be liable to the death penalty'. There was a further threat that 'All farmers, having sons in the F.S. Army, to clear out of this area 24 hours after blockades are removed.'[12]

One thing immediately sticks out from these notices: there was, in fact, no 3rd South Leitrim Brigade; there was only one South Leitrim Brigade. Ernie O'Malley records that this was made up of three battalions during the War of Independence and states that the flying column was disbanded after the 11 March 1921 disaster at Selton Hill near Mohill.[13]

John Charles Keegan did have some difficulty in identifying what unit he was attached to. In a letter to Éamon de Valera in March 1925, he stated that from 1922 until his arrest in March 1924 he was 'O/C VI Battalion, South Leitrim Brigade, III Division'.[14] In his IRA pension applications many years later, he would exhibit a similar confusion with ranks and units.[15] Is it possible that he was the one to write these notices? Or might he at least have had something to do with them?

On the morning the handwritten notices appeared, members of the clergy at some churches tore them down. One curate even told his parishioners after Mass that he would not run away; he would wait to be shot.[16] But in spite of such reassurance by the clergy, many in the South Leitrim community were very concerned at the prospect of the threats being put into effect. They were too well aware that only the previous Sunday a well-respected doctor in the locality had been gunned down in the streets of Mohill and, the following night, Edward Fitzgerald, a National Army soldier and a native of Mohill, had been shot in a pub in nearby Ballinamuck.

The notices served to increase the fear and terror people in the area were experiencing. They had, after all, appeared in the same month that had seen some of the worst excesses of attacks and reprisals in the Civil War. By this stage the anti-Treaty side had no prospect of victory and the conflict was descending into horror and counter-horror. A murderous trap-mine attack on National Army soldiers in Knocknagoshel, County Kerry, on 6 March was followed by the slaughter of anti-Treaty prisoners by elements of the

National Army the next day at Ballyseedy and Countess Bridge, and again two days later at Bahaghs Workhouse, all in County Kerry. As a result, the Leitrim notices, warning about deadly repercussions to any executions of anti-Treaty forces from the area, appear to have been taken extra seriously.

The people of South Leitrim did not have to wait long to have their worst fears realised. Another civilian, seventy-two-year-old Michael Reynolds, was shot dead on 30 April at his home just about five miles south of Mohill at Clooneagh. The gang had come knocking at 3 a.m. on the bedroom window of his son, John, who had previously been in the RIC but had resigned. His elderly father awoke, and when he refused a demand to open the front door, a shot was fired through it. Michael Reynolds fell back into his wife's arms crying out to his son, 'John, I'm shot, and done for.' John Reynolds responded by firing his own revolver, and the attackers dispersed.

Later investigation showed evidence of a sustained bullet and bomb attack on the house, with three bullet holes in the kitchen door alone. Dr Redahan of Mohill gave evidence at the subsequent inquest that Mr Reynolds' death was due to a gunshot wound, the bullet entering the mouth and passing on to the brain. Dr McGauran, who was also the coroner at Paddy Muldoon's inquest, stated that there was no doubt that Michael Reynolds had been murdered, but he would not suggest that it was a case of wilful murder. The jury returned a verdict of murder by some person or persons unknown.[17]

At this point, it should be noted that the anti-Treaty unit that John Charles Keegan was part of is recorded as having frequently used a safe house in Clooneagh during the Civil War period and so would have probably have known about John Reynolds' RIC background.[18]

***

Two weeks later, two brothers, Philip and Patrick McGuire, were shot and seriously wounded in their home, while their father suffered a minor gunshot wound.[19] The McGuire family lived at Gubbs near Cloone, which is only about a mile, as the crow flies, from Keegan's family home at Drumadorn.

On the night of Monday 14 May, the family were kneeling down saying the Rosary together, a common practice in Catholic homes at the time. At about 10 p.m. there was a knock on the door, and when Philip McGuire answered, he was confronted by a man in a belted coat, armed with a revolver. The armed man entered the house and, after confirming the identities of the occupants, called on Philip, who had served in the National Army, to follow him outside where there were others waiting. With that, Philip grabbed the intruder by an arm and by the belt of his coat, while at the same time his brother Patrick jumped to his assistance. The intruder fired off a number of shots, one piercing Patrick on his right side and another smashing through Philip's right jaw, exiting just under his temple.

As the badly wounded brothers fell to the ground, their

father came to their assistance, grappling with the gunman. Another shot rang out, grazing the elder McGuire's hand, but he showed tremendous courage and eventually succeeded in disarming his sons' attacker. A second intruder, who had entered the house while the struggle was in progress, hastily retreated when he saw the older man was now armed. The original gunman also made good his escape as Mr McGuire fired off a shot.

A relative of the family living nearby, having been informed of the dreadful attack, set off to secure medical aid and a priest. Before this assistance could arrive, the armed attackers returned and commenced firing at the house, demanding the return of the revolver. It was only when the gun was returned or thrown out to them that they finally departed the scene.

The attack on the McGuire family was reckless in the extreme and could easily have resulted in multiple fatalities. When the wounded members of the family were later taken to Carrick-on-Shannon hospital, there was initially little hope entertained for Patrick's recovery, while Philip's escape from death was regarded as almost miraculous in view of his serious head wound.

In the following days, National Army troops flooded into the area, setting up checkpoints in response to the latest attack.[20] This was on top of the investigations and searches that the two CID detectives from Dublin had carried out in the area earlier in the month in connection with Paddy Muldoon's murder. But the spate of violence was not yet over.

Just four days later another rural farming family, living not far from the Reynolds family of Clooneagh, were also to experience a tragic loss. On 18 May, twenty-seven-year-old Patrick Keville from Currycramp was taken from a neighbour's house and shot dead at the side of the road.

Similarly to Philip McGuire, Keville had served in the National Army, but he had resigned in January 1923 after the death of his brother from natural causes. On the day of his death, an armed gang had first called to Keville's father's house enquiring if his son Patrick was there. His sister informed them that he was visiting a neighbour's house nearby. The armed men asked to see his army discharge paper and she showed it to them. The gang then proceeded to the neighbour's house, called on Keville to come out, took him up to the main road and shot him dead. He received one revolver bullet through the head and two more 'in other parts of the body'.[21] Patrick Keville, a farmer's son and an ex-Free State officer, had been executed.

***

The church-gate warnings posted two months earlier had produced a deadly aftermath, and Keegan and his men certainly seemed to be at the centre of it all. A week after Keville's murder, the National Army in Longford was reporting to Athlone Command that 'The shooting of ex Lieut. Keville at Currycramp near Mohill on the night of the 18th inst., supposed to be the work of Keegan's Column.'[22]

There were indications many years later that Patrick Keville may have continued to engage in intelligence work for the National Army subsequent to his resignation. This might have accounted for Seán Mac Eoin writing in support of a compensation claim by Keville's sister that he was 'killed while a member of the forces and while on duty'.[23]

On 26 May, Commandant Luke Smyth, O/C 23rd Infantry Battalion, Longford, sent a detailed General Monthly Report for his area to his GOC in Athlone, Major General Mac Eoin. As well as giving his own opinion that Keegan was not right in his mind, it also stated 'Keegan has inside the present month shot 4 civilians, none of whom had any connection with our forces at time of shooting'.[24] Mac Eoin was now aware that the man he suspected of being the leader of the attack on Dr Muldoon was considered responsible for the murder of Patrick Keville and the wounding of the three McGuires.[25]

After the official ending of the Civil War in May 1923, there would be no further killings of civilians in the area that year. However, the National Army 'General Weekly Returns' for 'Irregular' activity in the 22nd and 23rd Battalion areas indicate that petty robbery and attacks on unarmed Civic Guards continued in the months following the ceasefire, with Keegan and his gang featuring prominently as suspects.

On 17 August 1923, nearly three months after the order to dump arms, the National Army were reporting to Athlone Command that 'a number of Irregulars were seen drilling around Cloone and Carrigallen with Keegan in charge'.[26] A week later, there is a report stating that 'four armed men raided a number of houses in Cloone, Co. Leitrim, and confined Civic Guards to Barracks while they were in the village'.[27] On 14 September, 'The postman plying between Carrigallen and Aughavas was held up and the letters examined, and three registered letters taken.'[28] Later, on 15 October, Carrigallen in Leitrim was again the target when the Civic Guards there were attacked 'and one of the Guards severely beaten'.[29] John Charles Keegan mentioned in his later pension applications that he was involved in two attacks on the Civic Guards in Carrigallen.

All the National Army reports name 'Keegan' as one of the principal leaders of the Irregulars in the 22nd Battalion's area. While John Charles' older brother, Michael Joe, was also active on the anti-Treaty side, John Charles himself claimed to be a leader of the local column.[30] In many of the National Army intelligence reports, 'Keegan' is named as a 'Principal Leader' alongside 'Farrell', i.e. Seán O'Farrell, who was mentioned by John Charles Keegan in his pension applications as his commandant.

Early the following year another attack took place which was chillingly reminiscent of that on the McGuire family. This time, however, it had fatal consequences.

On Wednesday 27 February 1924, the Lynch family of Drumliffen, near Gowel, were celebrating the marriage of their eldest son, James, with a party at their home.[31] Gowel is located about eleven miles northwest of Mohill. At 1.30 a.m. the following morning, with the wedding party in full swing, two armed men, in disguise, approached the Lynch residence while others waited further back. The bridegroom and his cousin, Patrick Lynch, went out to speak with them. When Patrick was told by the armed men that they wanted him to accompany them, he rushed back into the house. The two gunmen followed him in, ordering the frightened guests to put up their hands. James O'Brien, who had recently returned from America and was a brother of the bride, challenged the raiders. After he struck one of them, the raider in turn hit O'Brien forcibly over the head with a revolver butt and then shot him in the chest. Before the armed raiders departed, another guest asked one of them if he could fetch a priest and received the chilling reply, 'You may but you are too late.' Sure enough, by the time a doctor arrived shortly afterwards, James O'Brien was dead.

Again Dr Arthur McGauran was the coroner at the subsequent inquest and he said that he hoped they would be spared listening to such details again.[32] Yet another innocent had been attacked and shot dead in the coroner's area, by a gunman who had no hesitation in shooting defenceless civilians.

***

The murder of James O'Brien appears to have been the final straw. Just four days later, on 3 March 1924, Commandant

Patrick Woods received written orders, marked secret and confidential, from the chief of staff of the National Army. He had been placed in command of all military forces in the 'South Leitrim Special Military Area'.[33] South Leitrim had just been designated a Special Military Area due to its 'disturbed state'. Every effort was to be made to capture Keegan and his men, whether dead or alive.

Woods took up his duties two days later and based himself in Longford Barracks, which had been renamed Seán Connolly Barracks in honour of the dead Selton Hill leader. Woods was already aware 'that the disturbance in this area was due to the presence of about ten armed Irregulars under the leadership of John Charles Keegan, a deserter from the National Army'.[34]

Woods was familiar with the South Leitrim area. He had originally been sent to the locality the previous November and had spent until early January 1924 unsuccessfully attempting 'to effect the arrest of Keegan and others'. On that occasion he had searched the area 'by day and by night' but 'owing to the hostility of the inhabitants, mainly due through [sic] fear of Keegan and his gang, and their refusal to give any information regarding his movements, I was unable to effect their capture'. Commandant Woods, whose experience had marked him out for the task, had now returned to the same area with a specific mission. Keegan's reputation for being elusive was about to be tested again.

Woods set about organising a sting operation to capture Keegan, with help from Lieutenant Patrick Kane from

Abbeylara, County Longford.[35] The subsequent military inquiry into the circumstances of the operation would indicate exactly why John Charles Keegan's arrest was so sought after. Kane commanded the National Army garrison in Cloone and he had managed to gain the trust of many locals in an area where the populace was supportive of Keegan's men, either through fear or choice. The lieutenant pretended to be in sympathy with the anti-Treaty side and made it known that even if he had the opportunity to capture Keegan he wouldn't do it. This had the desired result and, on Friday 21 March 1924, Kane contacted Woods and told him that Keegan had taken the bait and wanted to meet him.

Keegan stated many years later that the meeting was for the purpose of him purchasing a machine gun.[36] Kane informed Woods that the arrangement was made through Henry Nicholl, who was related to both Keegan and Kane.[37] The meeting was to take place in the Nicholl family house at Rossan, a few miles south of Aughavas and near Keegan's family home at Drumadorn.

Kane suggested to Woods that the planned meeting would be an ideal opportunity for Woods and his men to capture Keegan. It was just over two weeks since Woods had been placed in charge of the South Leitrim Special Military Area. The prospect of capturing the – so far – elusive Keegan so quickly must have been tantalising. He told Kane to continue with his arrangements while he considered the matter further. Woods then went and put the plan before Major General

Mac Eoin, who was in Longford that same day. He told Mac Eoin that it would take a ruse like this to capture Keegan.[38]

Mac Eoin must have welcomed this long-awaited opportunity to apprehend the gunman who had caused death and destruction for over a year, as he immediately gave his permission, and full control of the operation, to the commandant. Woods met with Lieutenant Kane in Mohill the following day, Saturday, to tell him they had got the go-ahead, and in order to make their final plans.[39]

The meeting with Keegan had been set for 12 p.m. the following Monday, at the house of Patrick Nicholl, Henry Nicholl's father, as previously decided. Woods told Kane that he would arrive at the Nicholls' home at 1 a.m. on Tuesday morning with a unit of men and surround the house. Woods then exchanged his short .450 Webley revolver for Kane's Colt revolver, as the Webley would be easier for the lieutenant to conceal. Kane was to hold up Keegan in the house on the unit's arrival until Woods gained admittance, and he was to shoot him if he attempted to escape. Woods directed Kane, who would be in civilian clothes, to stay in the house during the operation – he was leaving nothing to chance.

On the Monday night Lieutenant Kane arrived at the Nicholls' house in Rossan as arranged and was accompanied by a schoolteacher from Cloone by the name of Curran.[40] Commandant Woods, with two other officers and two soldiers, arrived on the scene at 1 a.m. as previously agreed with Kane. Woods' unit had marched the six miles from

Carrigallen through the darkness, as the noise of approaching motorised transport might have given them away. They were led by Bernard Ward, a civilian from over the border in nearby Longford, who knew the location of the Nicholls' dwelling place.

Lieutenant Kane was having tea and was in discussion with Keegan as Woods placed his men in position around the house. He ordered Lieutenant Eugene Kilkenny to cover the back door and Driver J. Kelly to cover a gable window. Volunteer Patrick Collumb of the 8th Battalion, Athlone, was to keep watch at the front, while Captain Seán Moore of the 9th Battalion was to follow Woods through the front door after he had gained admittance. The guide, Bernard Ward, had taken shelter about 500 yards back from the house and Woods had given 'the usual orders to fire on any person attempting to flee from the house'.

When Woods banged on the door, which was locked, someone inside asked who was there. Woods replied, 'Military – open the door' and immediately two shots rang out.[41] Woods then heard the bolt being drawn back; he pushed the door open and saw a man he recognised as Keegan. He called on him to halt and when Keegan ran towards a room to the right, fired at him but missed.

As Woods entered the house in pursuit, he heard a burst of gunfire from the front of the house and the sound of breaking glass. The other officer in the party, Captain Moore, was armed with a machine gun. He broke in the front kitchen window, fired a burst of shots over Keegan's head and called on him to surrender. Yet, when cross-examined at the subsequent Court of Inquiry, Moore said, 'To the best of my belief no shots were fired inside the house except that [*sic*] fired by Comdt. Woods.'[42] He also said, 'When I first went to the window I saw a man leaving the house by the back door. This man was in dark civilian dress, at the same time I saw Keegan going from the direction of the back door towards the room.' When Keegan didn't surrender, Captain Moore moved around to the window of the room into which Keegan had fled, and fired another burst into that room when he saw Keegan trying to escape from it. Then Lieutenant Kilkenny and the two soldiers informed Moore that there was a man shot at the back of the house.

Meanwhile Woods was shouting orders from inside the house, telling them to cease fire while he again called on Keegan to surrender. Finally Keegan called out, 'I will surrender', and Woods ordered him to come out of the room and step into the kitchen. When Keegan did so, Woods had him handcuffed and searched, but no arms were found in his possession.[43] Woods was then informed by Kelly that there was a man shot outside and he went out to find Lieutenant Kane lying about two yards from the back door.

Woods examined the body of his colleague and found he had been shot through the head. The commandant and his four men stood for a short time to pray over their fallen comrade while John Charles Keegan stood handcuffed beside them. Kane's body was then carried into the kitchen where Woods removed the short Webley revolver from the deceased's pocket. It was fully loaded.

The commandant searched the room that Keegan had taken refuge in but did not search the rest of the house. Neither did he search Curran, or Patrick Nicholl and his family, who had been in other rooms, some upstairs, during the shoot-out. Having captured Keegan, the commandant thought it wise not to delay in the area with only a small unit of men in case Keegan's gang unexpectedly turned up. He ordered his men to take the prisoner to Carrigallen Barracks. Later that night, Kane's body was removed to Longford Barracks. It seems he had been shot by his own men as he fled the house from an armed and dangerous Keegan.

After Commandant Woods had returned to his Longford base, he sent a brief report direct to the chief of staff in Dublin and a copy of this to Mac Eoin. He informed them 'that John Charles Keegan the notorious Irregular leader in County Leitrim was arrested by me at 1 a.m. this morning in Rossan near Carrigallen'. He made no reference to the operation other than to mention that 'Lieut. P. J. Kane was shot whilst arrest was being effected' and that a detailed report would follow.[44]

This was a big breakthrough in the National Army's efforts to bring an end to what could only be described as banditry in South Leitrim. That same day, reflecting the importance of the news and following receipt of a radio message from Athlone

Command, an urgent report went out from the Office of the Director of Intelligence in Dublin to a number of senior figures.[45] These included General O'Duffy, now the minister for defence, the attorney general and the commissioner of the Civic Guard. They were made aware 'that JOHN CHARLES KEEGAN [*sic*]' who had been 'badly wanted for sometime, was captured' and that Lieutenant P. J. Kane was killed in the operation. A warrant for the detention of Keegan under the Public Safety Act was being prepared.

The report also mentioned that 'Keegan is wanted for a number of murders, particularly the murder of 2nd Lieut. Pat Keville on the 18/5/23' and that his file was being forwarded to the Civic Guard 'with a view to the institution of Civil proceedings, if possible'. The urgent report concluded by saying that as the captured man 'has a number of dangerous accomplices it is recommended that the Adjutant General arrange for his immediate removal to Dublin or the Curragh, until such time as the Civil authorities are prepared to take him over'.

The very next day, at 7.15 p.m., John Charles Keegan was handed over into the custody of the military governor of Arbour Hill Detention Barracks in Dublin, where Éamon de Valera and Austin Stack were the only other prisoners being held. The National Army had finally gotten Leitrim's most sought-after criminal, a suspect for the deaths of a number of unarmed civilians, into secure detention.

***

All of the newspaper reports on the happenings at Rossan on the morning of 25 March referred to John Charles Keegan as a 'wanted' or 'much wanted' man, but they also emphasised the fact that he was once in the National Army. The newspapers uniformly portrayed Keegan as a bandit, or renegade, on the run.[46]

When Commandant Woods met his superior officer, Major General Mac Eoin, to obtain permission to go ahead with Lieutenant Kane's plan, he told Mac Eoin that 'if Keegan was arrested conditions in Leitrim would return to normal'.[47] Woods, it turned out, was proven correct. Ten months after the Civil War ceasefire, and with Keegan in Arbour Hill Prison, the banditry that had characterised the Mohill, Cloone and Aughavas areas finally petered out, replaced by a peace that was longed for by all the community, other than those few desperate individuals with a personal interest in ongoing disorder.

There were no charges brought against John Charles Keegan while he was imprisoned in Arbour Hill. Instead it appears from his initial pension application that he was released from military arrest as part of the general amnesty of November 1924.[48] The Free State government had followed up 1923 legislation that provided an indemnity for its own forces with an Act of General Amnesty for all prisoners. It may have been the case that the authorities could find no civilians from the South Leitrim area prepared to give evidence against Keegan, just as National Army intelligence had suggested in May 1923.[49]

However, immediately after his release, the Civic Guard took a case against Keegan, and he and Joseph Clyne were found guilty at the Central Criminal Court in Dublin 'of having in 1923 assaulted and obstructed three Civic Guards in the exercise of their duty in Cloone, Leitrim'.[50] In this instance, they had held up the unarmed Guards and brandished revolvers in their faces.

Both defendants refused to recognise the court and were remanded in custody, pending sentencing. Keegan stated in his pension application that he was subsequently sentenced to a mere six months in Mountjoy Prison.

CHAPTER 15

Fr Edward Ryans' fortunes had changed dramatically over the course of 1923. When finally released from Mountjoy Prison in December, he was faced with the ignominy of moving back into the family home, Knockranny House in Keadue. There he was living with his parents in what he described as 'rather difficult circumstances' with his only income being 'an occasional mass offering'.[1]

Ryans had not been pursued in connection with Paddy Muldoon's murder or the military's charges against him in the aftermath of the Civil War. However, he could not argue for a new appointment while the Muldoon affair was still outstanding, as Bishop Hoare would only remind him 'that the whole country believes that I am a murderer'. The bishop was also claiming that the authorities had written to him saying that Ryans was released on condition that he clear out of the country at once.[2]

It was against this background that Fr Ryans decided to approach the IRA, early in 1924, requesting that they hold an inquiry into Dr Muldoon's killing with a view to exonerating him from any involvement. An investigation was agreed to at the highest levels of the IRA and was carried out by Frank O'Beirne, officer commanding the 3rd Western Division, who was based in Sligo.

It would seem that the three men who had taken part in the attack on Dr Muldoon were interviewed, probably having been identified by their commandant, Seán O'Farrell, or the quartermaster who was reported to have armed them on the night. Following this, a press release was prepared, which Ryans was allowed to view before it was sent to IRA General Headquarters in Dublin for release.[3] O'Beirne also enquired of headquarters 'if a short paragraph stating regrets or sympathy to relations should be added'.[4]

After IRA Chief of Staff Frank Aiken had sought some clarification from O'Beirne, and minor alterations to the text were made, the press release was issued on 15 May in the name of the publicity department, Irish Republican Army, General Headquarters, Dublin. Copies of the statement were sent to a number of publications, including the *Longford Leader, Irish Independent, The Irish Times* and *The Freeman's Journal*.[5]

This public announcement from the anti-Treaty forces commenced by saying that it was entirely untrue 'that a certain civilian was responsible for the death of Dr Muldoon'. The IRA statement did not name the civilian it was alluding to but went on to give what it considered the 'facts of the shooting'. Its version of the events stated that a party of armed IRA Volunteers were detailed to enter Mohill on the night of 18 March 1923 'for the purpose of ambushing a Free State patrol'. When this unit had been in position for some time 'two men wearing trench coats appeared and, on being ordered to halt they took to flight'. The press release goes on to say that due to this refusal to halt, their men came to the conclusion that they were 'Staters in mufti' (Free State soldiers in civilian attire) 'and opened fire on them'. The IRA statement concluded that Dr Muldoon's death was very much regretted by the Volunteers involved, but the subsequent inquiry proved to the satisfaction of their superior officers that it was 'an unavoidable accident'.[6]

Rita Muldoon was so incensed by the contents of the IRA's statement that she telegraphed the press on the day of publication. The doctor's widow bluntly and bravely stated, 'My husband's death was not the result of an unavoidable accident, but a carefully planned, cruel, callous murder.'[7] She would follow this immediate denial with a detailed rebuttal of the IRA press release, which she felt had trivialised her husband's murder. The *Longford Leader* newspaper carried her well-crafted and carefully thought out rebuttal three weeks later.[8]

First, she dealt with the issue of the clothes worn by Paddy that night. The statement claimed that Paddy was wearing a trench coat and was identified as a 'Stater in Mufti'. Rita said that her husband was in fact wearing a light-grey lounge suit on the night; he wasn't wearing an overcoat of any kind and neither was his companion, Mr Geelan. She was well qualified to confirm what her husband wore on the night, as she was there when his lifeless body was carried back to their house.

Rita went on to quote all of Mr Geelan's evidence from the inquest, which specifically mentioned that 'No warning was given before the shot was fired.' Furthermore, on what was a bright night with a street light nearby, two gunmen continued shooting, but only at Dr Muldoon, after his identification was confirmed by his companion naming him. Crucially, Rita then described the cause of her husband's death: 'The position of the fatal and only wound under his right collar bone proves profoundly that he was shot at the point of the rifle and not while running away.'[9]

As her husband's post-mortem examination was carried out in their family home, and as she had retained the shirt he had been wearing, Rita was writing with authority on what was a very difficult subject for her. Her husband's death certificate supports the claim that he was shot in the upper chest, as does the report of Inspector Breen of the Civic Guard, who attended the inquest and would have viewed the body.[10]

Rita Muldoon also questioned the fourteen-month delay in the IRA issuing their publicity statement, and asked who the 'certain civilian' that the statement sought to exonerate was. She also questioned the organisation's motive for 'trying to veneer' the conduct of this civilian believed responsible for the callous and brutal murder of her husband. She asked why he himself (Ryans) didn't take 'appropriate action in the proper place against those who have published the statement that he is responsible for the murder, with a view to having his character vindicated'.

In a telling comment, Rita picked up on Bishop Hoare's biblical theme and asked, 'Why be branded – if not guilty – with the Sin of Cain'? She may have been alluding to the bishop's letter of a year earlier, but, unlike him, she would not be satisfied with her husband's murderer being banished; she wanted justice, not penitence.

Rita then questioned the coincidence of the timing of the Sunday night ambush of 'Staters in Mufti' with her husband's custom, 'well known to many', of visiting his friend Canon Masterson's house on Sunday evenings. Her conclusion was that her husband's death was not an unavoidable accident but a carefully planned assassination, not carried out for any political reason, although 'political ends were probably used'.[11]

Rita's letter in the paper ended with the question: 'Were the three young men who committed the murder prompted and urged to do so by this civilian with a view to personal revenge or suppression of previous iniquities?'

An earlier handwritten draft of Rita Muldoon's response and a copy of the typed letter still exist. In the typewritten copy there is a final sentence that is scored out and was not used in the publicised version. It reads: 'It was publicly stated that the murder of my husband was due to the act of a foreigner and an apostate.'[12] Edward Ryans was born in England and had changed allegiance in the Civil War; he went from speaking publicly in support of the Treaty to being an active anti-Treaty supporter.[13] As she had been on the night of her husband's death, Rita Muldoon was clearly still convinced of Edward Ryans' culpability in the death of her husband.

This was a remarkable letter from the widow of an innocent victim, particularly when considered against what was happening both in Ireland and in Rita's own private life at the time. She was taking on the publicity department of one of the two recently warring armies in a country still bitterly divided. She was not prepared to allow Edward Ryans to escape the responsibility of his actions and return to public life without being taken to task. As well as taking on the IRA, and rearing four young children, Rita was also grieving for her widowed mother, who had died on 3 June 1924, just days before the publication of her letter. However, despite these issues, she had successfully and fearlessly demolished the account of her husband's murder put forward by the IRA. They were to make no further public comment that year.

***

Given that the statement aimed to clear Ryans' name, the IRA publicity department's press release of May 1924 proved a disaster for Fr Edward Ryans. He wrote to IRA Chief of Staff Frank Aiken shortly after Rita Muldoon's rebuttal was published. He tried to explain how Frank O'Beirne, the IRA commander, had gotten it all wrong before the statement was issued (in spite of Ryans being allowed to see the document in advance). Ryans now claimed:

> That statement published has absolutely ruined me, and has confirmed the belief that I am the perpetrator or the instigator of that shooting. That statement, containing untruths as it did, is regarded by the public as a stunt …

His own attempt to clear himself of suspicion had failed. But Ryans goes on:

> Now O'Beirne suggests that GHQ send down a man, an expert, to enquire into the whole thing and clear it up. What evidence does anybody want. The three men did the shooting. They admit it … Further enquiry is only tomfoolery. Surely GHQ might be able to devise some means of clearing me. That half-bred statement that appeared in the press which was so easily rebutted by Mrs Muldoon makes the clearing up somewhat more difficult but the whole thing is such a shocking injustice to me that I beg of you to make a strong endeavour to clear my name of it.

The tone of the letter suggests Ryans considered himself an insider trying to get his superiors to 'fix' his situation and clear his name – not by investigating, but by issuing some sort of formal statement.[14]

Despite Ryans' desire to avoid any reopening of the IRA inquiry, Aiken took a different approach one month later and 'sent a Staff Officer down to investigate the whole affair'.[15] The officer called to the priest's home place in Keadue to interview him, only to learn that Ryans was away in England.

Fr Ryans heard nothing further following the July 1924 visit of the IRA staff officer to Leitrim. The following November the government decided on an amnesty for all acts committed by either side between the signing of the Treaty in December 1921 and May 1923. This effectively ended any chance of a trial for anyone connected with the murder of Paddy Muldoon.

Despite the amnesty, however, the allegations still stuck to Ryans. On 17 January 1925 he wrote a seven-page letter to Sinn Féin President Éamon de Valera, asking him to help clear his name.[16] Most of this letter is a detailed account of how, after his release from prison in December 1923, Ryans pursued the IRA locally and centrally to issue a statement acknowledging responsibility for Dr Muldoon's death, thereby clearing his name.[17] Ryans admitted to de Valera that he was shown the details of the IRA publicity department's May 1924 statement in advance and was asked if its publication would satisfy him. He told de Valera, rather unconvincingly, that he was more interested in who would sign the statement than the details it contained, which he 'could not criticise'. When told that the statement would go out over the name of Frank Aiken, IRA chief of staff, he was satisfied that 'even a prejudiced public would be quite assured' that Aiken would not take on such responsibility on behalf of the IRA unless Ryans was absolutely innocent.

The document subsequently published, although 'some-what similar' to what he was shown, was not signed by Aiken. Ryans informed de Valera that instead of clearing him, the document had only damned him when Rita Muldoon 'at once showed the details of that document to be merely a fabrication'. This rendered the IRA document worthless and had in fact strengthened her contention that 'he was murdered by me or for me'. Furthermore, in the absence of an IRA response to the widow's contradictions, Ryans maintained that the net result was 'the whole public now believes that I am guilty'.[18]

Fr Ryans described to de Valera his difficult living conditions and financial position. He explained that Bishop Hoare told him, on his release from prison, that the Free State authorities had written to the bishop saying he was being released on condition that he cleared out of the country. Ryans informed de Valera that he was of the opinion that the authorities and his bishop were possibly in league to make this happen. He also suggested that if he tried to argue with the bishop for a new appointment locally, he would 'be told that the whole country believes I am a murderer'. He also confided to de Valera that his difficult relationship with Bishop Hoare went back to the South Longford by-election of May 1917 and that ever since the bishop 'has been persecuting me'.

At this stage, it should be pointed out that Ryans' description of his difficult situation was solely concerned with his loss of position and income, and with clearing his name. While he claimed that he was being deprived of a livelihood by his superior's attitude, there was no mention of any sense of personal or spiritual loss from being prevented from carrying out his priestly calling. Unlike in his correspondence with Seán Mac Eoin, Ryans avoided any details of his young housekeeper's pregnancy and the subsequent child abandonment charge. All he said to de Valera was that the Free State authorities 'were prosecuting an absurd charge' against him, which fell through after three 'vindictive' trials in Dublin. He claimed the CID 'invented theories' connecting him to Dr Muldoon's shooting with the result that he spent eight months in prison. Ryans told de Valera that, over the course of a three-month investigation, the Free State police and military drummed these theories into the public conscience and were actually about to put him forward on a murder charge.

In this letter Edward Ryans also managed to change the narrative of his past by giving a very different version of his Civil War activities than he had given to Major General Mac Eoin two years earlier. Ryans' habit of altering the truth to suit his purpose was once again evident as he suggested to the Sinn Féin president that he might know who he was as he had done 'plenty of work for the boys in the Black & Tan times' and 'also in the recent war'.[19] By way of example he recounted the seizure of his car, valued at £500, by the Free State forces 'because I drove to safety Tom Kearney [sic], McEvilly etc. who escaped from Longford Prison [sic]'. This was the jailbreak that John Charles Keegan had been central to and which led to his court martial and death sentence.

Ryans involvement in assisting some of the prisoners to make good their escape was testified to many years later by the aforementioned Tom Carney.[20] Carney was active on the anti-Treaty side in the Civil War. He was born in Kiltimagh, County Mayo in 1891 and spent five years in the RIC before joining the IRA in 1921. His police experience was not wasted, as he later served as an intelligence officer in the IRA's East Mayo Brigade. He was captured in August 1922 by the National Army. While imprisoned in Longford Barracks, he took part in the mass escape of November 1922.

In the 1950s Carney was one of many old IRA men, mainly from the anti-Treaty side, who gave statements of their activities to Ernie O'Malley. He confirmed Keegan's involvement in the Longford Barracks breakout, but gave him a more minor role than Keegan's own pension application recollections had suggested.[21] Carney told O'Malley that, after their escape, he and others made their way north, on foot, to Leitrim, with the help of republican sympathisers along the way. They were directed to a sympathiser in Aughavas, just across the border from Longford, who put them in contact with Fr Ryans, who was of course the local curate. Ryans undertook to drive them to his father's house in Arigna, County Roscommon. Before setting off Ryans asked the escapees, who were armed, 'But if I'm held up what you will do [sic]?' before answering his own rhetorical question: 'Let ye blaze like hell.'[22]

Carney's account of Edward Ryans as someone willing to provide transport for gunmen and be a party to their violence, if necessary, happened just four months before the priest's involvement in driving Paddy Muldoon's killers into Mohill.[23] As it happened, in that instance Carney and his fellow escapees made their way to Fr Ryans' father's house in Arigna without the need of firearms. From there they continued their escape, on foot, southwest to Ballaghaderreen.

In the course of his time in Leitrim and Arigna, Carney, the RIC man turned IRA intelligence officer, picked up some information about the helpful priest. He was able to tell O'Malley that Ryans had a housekeeper who got into trouble and that the local view was that he had asked his brother to assume responsibility for the child, but his brother refused.[24] Carney also had a version of the abandonment in which the housekeeper and a 'gentleman' were arrested by the police. He is another source for a potential motive for the murder. His account described Dr Muldoon as a prominent republican whom Fr Ryans had approached to perform an illegal operation on the girl, but who had refused to do so.

Ryans' affirmation of his anti-Treaty activities to de Valera contradicts his earlier emphatic denials of anti-Treaty involvement to Major General Mac Eoin and to Bishop Hoare. He went on to tell de Valera that he complained to Frank O'Beirne, O/C 3rd Western Division, that the published 'document did me harm & not good'.[25] However, O'Beirne responded to the priest's ongoing requests by telling him in writing that 'he was heartily sick of the whole business'.[26] Ryans told de Valera that O'Beirne's frustration was based on the belief that Ryans was insisting the only means of clearing him was for the IRA to publish 'the names of the 3 men implicated in the shooting'. Ryans insisted that this wasn't the case; instead, he told de Valera, it was actually

Robert (Bob) Brennan of the IRA publicity department who 'said to me that he could see no other way out of it'.

In appealing to the president of Sinn Féin to intervene on his behalf, Fr Ryans admitted it was really a matter for the IRA, but he had failed to get them 'to do what they obviously should do in the matter'.[27]

After reading Fr Ryans' long letter, de Valera must have been left puzzled as to what the priest thought he could do to assist him. After all, Ryans had been given the opportunity to approve the original statement issued by the IRA publicity department before it was published. The suggestion that if it had gone out with the name of Chief of Staff Frank Aiken attached the Irish public would have been assured that the priest was innocent, seemed, at the very least, slightly delusional. Aiken was not a figure of such importance or trust to Irish people at that point in time.

Before responding to Ryans' letter, de Valera's secretary sent a written request for all the particulars of the case to Bob Brennan, the IRA's director of publicity. Brennan returned the typed request with a penned note attached. It confirmed that he had met Ryans before the May 1924 statement to the media, had taken a statement from the priest and given it to Aiken, 'who said he would look into the matter'. Brennan said he did not issue the May 1924 publicity statement and that it was issued without his knowledge.[28]

Then, on 22 January 1925, Frank Aiken himself wrote a detailed letter to de Valera setting out his involvement in the press statement.[29] He mentioned that he had received a report from Bob Brennan saying Fr Ryans was accused of Dr Muldoon's murder and 'wanted us to clear him of it'. Aiken said that he then asked Frank O'Beirne, OC, 3rd Western Division of the anti-Treaty IRA, to investigate the case and report back. On receipt of this report Aiken himself drew up a statement which O'Beirne confirmed was true in every detail and, apparently without involving Bob Brennan, his director of publicity, Aiken himself issued it to the press from the 'Army publicity department'.

Aiken told de Valera that his attitude to the matter was 'that even if Fr Ryan [*sic*] were guilty of the first charge', presumably referring to him fathering his housekeeper's baby, 'we should not allow him to be wrongly accused of the shooting of Dr Muldoon'. However, Rita Muldoon's public response had contradicted so much of Aiken's statement, it suggested that the IRA was trying to shield Ryans. Aiken told de Valera that, following receipt of a letter of complaint from Fr Ryans, he had sent a staff officer down to the Leitrim area in late July 1924 to investigate the whole affair on his behalf. The chief of staff enclosed a copy of that officer's report, which was simply signed 'K', with his letter to de Valera.

CHAPTER 16

The IRA intelligence report sent to de Valera by Aiken was signed with a simple letter 'K' for good reason. Both sides in the Civil War had operated intelligence units. Intelligence-gathering methods were reasonably sophisticated for the time and played an important role in the conflict. Although the Civil War had officially ended more than a year before, the IRA continued to exist and operate as the political situation in Ireland continued to evolve. 'K' would therefore have been compromised at that point by his identity being revealed.

The report to his chief of staff, dated Saturday 26 July 1924, was compiled just over two months after Rita Muldoon's response to the IRA press statement. The detailed two-and-a-half page handwritten report began with K's account of how he had spent the 'worst five days' ever on 'an absolute crock' of a borrowed motorbike 'switch backing' over the mountains of Leitrim.[1] Being a staff officer in a recently defeated army was evidently not a comfortable position.

He then said that he had no results to report, as he had been sent to Leitrim before proper arrangements were put in place. He explained that Rita Muldoon was now living in Clifden and if she was to be interviewed, someone else would have to travel to Galway. Furthermore, he and Frank O'Beirne, OC, 3rd Western Division, had journeyed to Keadue only to learn that Fr Ryans was away in England. They also failed to meet and interview the party of three men who had carried out the attack on Paddy Muldoon. Two of the three were imprisoned, one only recently (most likely referring to John Charles Keegan's situation, as he had been captured at Rossan by the National Army in March). The third member of the gang was still at liberty, but as they could not locate Seán O'Farrell, the brigade OC, they decided against wasting time trying to find him.

K reported that he learned no new information about the case, which from all accounts was 'exceedingly difficult and complex'. However, one thing on which he felt 'personally convinced was that Ryan [*sic*] is a "bad lot"' and that he was the only one 'who has kept this matter alive by his persistency'. He also felt that the possibility of eliciting the true facts was very remote and his recommendation was to let the case drop altogether.

K's report recommended to Aiken that the IRA should get over the Ryans difficulty by telling the priest 'straight out to clear himself publicly of the first charge', which presumably was that he was the father of Mary Kate Gallogly's now deceased child. If Ryans were to do this, K felt that the second charge, responsibility for Dr Muldoon's murder, 'which hinged on it would then fall flat'. Despite this recommendation, and although he hadn't met Fr Ryans on this trip, K felt able to say of Ryans: 'He is very reluctant to refer to or discuss the first charge of which he is undoubtedly guilty and there are certainly grounds for suspecting him of the second.'

K's travelling companion, Frank O'Beirne, had overseen the earlier IRA investigation into Paddy Muldoon's death that preceded the IRA statement to the press. It was also O'Beirne who had later told Ryans that he was sick of the whole matter. It seems likely that O'Beirne's view of Ryans, and what he learned through the IRA investigation and subsequent dealings with him, formed most of K's opinion in the report, which was a damning assessment of Ryans from two anti-Treaty comrades who were aware of much of the background to Dr Muldoon's killing.

K's final comment to Aiken about the priest was that 'Anyhow an individual like him deserves scant consideration.' He then summarised the IRA's options as letting the case drop or holding over the inquiry until all three of the men involved in the attack were available. If Aiken were to opt for the renewed investigation, K told him to devote at least ten days and a car to do the job, and to have all arrangements in place beforehand. He obviously did not want to repeat the motorbike journey to Leitrim searching out unavailable individuals.

Recent handwriting comparisons have conclusively identified the decisive IRA staff officer K as none other than Seán Lemass.[2] Lemass was to follow de Valera as Ireland's Taoiseach in 1959 and is generally regarded as the father of Irish industrial and commercial expansion. He is also remembered as being an extremely straight individual who expected the same straightness from others.[3] An individual of Fr Ryans' self-serving disposition was unlikely to receive much consideration from someone of the character of Seán Lemass.

It would seem that de Valera decided to go with Aiken's advice and await the outcome of any further investigation. On 27 January 1925, after receipt of the IRA chief's advice, de Valera's secretary wrote an extremely short response to Ryans, acknowledging receipt of the priest's long letter. He was then simply informed that the Sinn Féin president had referred the matter 'to the Chief of Staff for consideration and report'.[4] This curt response would have allowed a period of time for any renewed investigation.

However, plans for this latest investigation were interrupted when the murder of Paddy Muldoon burst back into the national news the following month, on this occasion impacting on the republicans' electoral efforts.

***

On 27 February 1925 the *Irish Independent* reported that, once again, they had received a telegram from Mrs Muldoon of Clifden. The telegram referred to the newspaper's earlier reports of a statement regarding the shooting of her husband, made by Frank O'Beirne, the high-ranking IRA officer who was now standing as one of the republican candidates in the 1925 Sligo–Leitrim by-election.

A republican election rally had been organised for O'Beirne in Mohill just prior to Rita sending this telegram. The opening speech was made by Fr Michael O'Flanagan, the staunch republican priest that Fr Edward Ryans had been compared with during the South Longford by-election of 1917, and who, like Ryans, had taken the anti-Treaty side in the Civil War.

As he worked the crowd up for the main speaker, Fr O'Flanagan was interrupted by William Murphy, a cousin of Paddy Muldoon. Murphy shouted from the crowd for the priest to ask O'Beirne: 'Who shot Dr Muldoon here in Mohill, the best and truest man ever was in the world.' Fr O'Flanagan responded that he had never heard of Dr Muldoon.[5] O'Flanagan had just returned to Ireland after an absence of over three years, which he'd spent promoting the anti-Treaty cause in America and Australia.[6]

Murphy's interruption provoked an angry response from some in the crowd, and Fr O'Flanagan stepped down from the platform to calm matters down and usher Murphy away. However, the papers went on to report that the candidate who spoke after the priest, Frank O'Beirne, said he would like to answer Murphy's earlier question. O'Beirne stated that he was still an officer in the IRA and confirmed that he had been involved in that group's inquiry into the shooting. He went on to repeat the line that Paddy Muldoon was shot by anti-Treaty forces because they thought he was a Free State officer in plain clothes. O'Beirne reiterated the claim that the doctor had been shot by mistake and that 'the Republican Army had nothing against him and we are all sorry he was shot'.[7]

This was a very half-hearted apology, at best, for the killing of an innocent man who had been sympathetic to the republican movement during the War of Independence. It was also rehashing the mistaken-identity excuse that Rita Muldoon had previously shown to be completely false. Prior to O'Beirne's comments, the IRA had not made any public response to Rita Muldoon's rebuttal of the press release of the previous year. It must have been very distressing for her, therefore, to have a republican candidate and serving IRA officer publicly repeating the same false account of her husband's death on the very streets where he was gunned down. It was likely this distress that led to her sending the telegram to the *Irish Independent*.

Rita's telegram to the *Independent* dismissed O'Beirne's statement at Mohill as a complete fabrication and asked why she, the widow, was not notified of the alleged investigation.[8] She followed up the telegram a week later with a full reply to O'Beirne's claims, querying why he never responded to her published response to the IRA statement issued the previous year.

With the Civil War now over, she questioned why he could not publish the full facts of the IRA's investigation. Rita reminded the readers of the evidence given by Edward Geelan about the attack on her husband, and mentioned how peculiar it was that Mr Geelan wasn't mistaken for a Free State soldier.[9]

At this point, Rita wasn't the only family member agitating for answers. A few days after her telegram to the *Irish Independent*, her brother Ambrose wrote to the department of justice regarding the correspondence that had appeared in the paper concerning his brother-in-law's murder. Frank O'Beirne had publicly admitted his involvement in the IRA investigation and inferred that he had knowledge of the attackers involved in a still unsolved murder case. The assistant secretary of the department wrote back on behalf of the minister for justice, stating that the matter was under investigation.[10]

***

Less than three weeks later, on 18 March 1925, the second anniversary of Dr Muldoon's death, John Charles Keegan was writing to Éamon de Valera, seeking his assistance. Keegan had been released from military detention in Arbour Hill Prison, where he had been imprisoned after his arrest at Rossan in March 1924, at the same time as de Valera.

In the now somewhat common practice of lower-ranked comrades appealing for assistance to the higher ranks, he began his letter to de Valera with a full account of his own seven-year career with the IRA. He was very particular in describing how, virtually on his own, he arranged the mass breakout from Longford Barracks in November 1922, freeing about seventy anti-Treaty captives and taking eleven rifles and 500 rounds of ammunition. This description, it should be noted, did not altogether concur with Tom Carney's later account of the escape.

Keegan went on to tell the Sinn Féin president that he could not understand 'the position I am fixed in presently'. He was not happy with the 'quick decisions' of some of his superior officers and he now wanted 'a full inquiry made into his case'. He was adamant that he 'served away under orders from the Irish Republican headquarters' and 'Every order that was issued from headquarters I carried out to the letter.' He ended the letter with the comment, 'I am guilty of no offence for such actions that I have already been informed about' and signed it 'Comdt Keegan, South L[eitrim] Bde'.[11]

It is likely that Keegan's appeal to de Valera was made as a direct result of a renewed investigation by the IRA into Paddy Muldoon's murder. Many years later, in his applications for an IRA pension or special allowance, Keegan referred to meeting de Valera after being released from Arbour Hill. He said that de Valera had asked him to fill out a report on all his IRA activities. Keegan completed a report as requested and provided it 'personally to President de Valera'.[12] If that were the case, de Valera now found himself in a very difficult position: how to satisfy the opposing interests of Ryans and the man who had shared his own incarceration in Arbour Hill Prison. Keegan's repeated reference to following orders appears to imply that he was not prepared to accept responsibility for Dr Muldoon's death other than on the grounds that he was acting under orders.

In addition, Rita Muldoon's recent second public inter-vention was a timely reminder that she would challenge any new public statement by the IRA categorising her husband's killing as an 'unavoidable accident', or any attempt to exo-nerate Ryans. This almost certainly left the renewed investi-gation in a quandary.

Seán Lemass had suggested, in his July 1924 'K' report to Aiken, that perhaps 'the best course would be to let the case drop and so obviate the difficulty of reconciling contradictory statements and untying a black knot'.[13] After all, there was no possibility that the previous 'unfortunate accident' conclusion could be relied upon to go unchallenged if it was used again. Rita Muldoon's public response had shown that to be lies. Furthermore, the notion of the killing being an accident had also been dismissed within the IRA, on the strength of Seán Lemass' subsequent report.

And so, belatedly following Lemass' advice, the matter – as well as the latest investigation – was allowed to drop. No further statement was ever issued by the IRA to exonerate Fr Ryans or excuse those who had carried out the actual attack on Paddy Muldoon. Rita's courageous public response to both Aiken's botched press release and O'Beirne's comments, made in the heat of an election rally in Mohill, went unchallenged. Keegan's letter to Éamon de Valera, claiming he carried out orders to the letter, is the last insight into the IRA's investigations.

Rita Muldoon, it seemed, had faced down the IRA's public pronouncements and had the final word on the truth behind her husband's murder. Edward Ryans' final attempt at public exoneration had come to nothing. Ryans, and to a lesser extent John Charles Keegan and the other two assailants, were left exposed by the republican movement's silence.

***

In or around April 1925 there were reports of an arms dump uncovered in the Arigna Mountains area of North Roscommon by Free State forces.[14] Further searches of the area followed, with arms seized and men arrested, including Fr Ryans. Once again, the priest found himself in trouble with the law.

In early July Ryans and two other men appeared at Boyle courthouse in County Roscommon to face charges of possession of arms or explosives. Armed detectives made a dramatic appearance at the courthouse showing off rifles, revolvers and explosives that had been discovered during searches in the Keadue and Fostia areas.

Ryans was first up, facing a charge of having two rifles at his residence. When they were found, his sister Margaret claimed to have no knowledge of their presence. Sergeant P. Corry testified that he found the rifles in good condition, wrapped in an overcoat in a loft fifteen yards from the dwelling house.

Ryans' defence was a denial of any knowledge of the rifles. He did not give evidence himself, but his solicitor, Mr Pettit, said on his behalf 'that he had nothing to do with the people who had these rifles', that the district had been overrun by Irregulars and that the defendant's brother, who had since left the country, had been one of their leaders.[15]

A statement from Ryans' solicitor denied that his client had any involvement with the anti-Treaty forces during the Civil War. Yet again Ryans was blaming matters on his brother, even though a newspaper report in April 1923 had stated that Vincent had handed in his weapons to the National Army when he surrendered.[16] Many years later, Margaret McKeon, Ryans' sister who had also claimed to have no knowledge of the weapons, would state that she kept arms and ammunition for the Arigna anti-Treaty unit during the Civil War period.[17]

This time Ryans' word was accepted by the court. The charges for possession of arms, ammunition and explosives against both him and the two other defendants were dismissed. Unlike Ryans, they had both given evidence in person. Vincent's departure from Ireland had made him the perfect scapegoat, both for the arms charges and, arguably, for Fr Ryans' previous predicament, as it would have given Edward the opportunity to go back to Bishop Hoare and tell him, as he had previously told Seán Mac Eoin, that Vincent was the father of Mary Kate's child, without fear of contradiction. However, if he did attempt to promote that version of events to his superior at this late stage, it doesn't appear to have changed Bishop Hoare's opinion of him, or his superior's understanding of what actually happened.

In fact, this arms charge appears to have been the final straw for Ryans, who seemingly had come to the realisation that the IRA's renewed investigation was not going to clear him of involvement in Paddy Muldoon's murder, or change the bishop's perception of him. If anything, he was more sure than ever that both State and Church wanted him gone. Exhausted from fighting a losing battle, he finally decided to give them what they wanted and began to set things in motion for leaving the country.

On 17 June, in the period between Ryans' arrest and court appearance, Canon Patrick Donohoe of St Mary's, Granard, wrote to Seán Mac Eoin asking if he could intercede on Fr Ryans' behalf in obtaining monetary compensation for his car. This was the same car that Ryans had written to Mac Eoin about while in Mountjoy Prison. Without any introduction, the canon launched straight into the purpose of his letter, telling Mac Eoin that 'Father Ryans has consented to go to America but claims he is entitled to compensation for the loss of a very valuable motor car seized by the military.'

Canon Donohoe was the brother of Mrs Flynn of Aughavas, and thus a member of the family Ryans stayed with when he was on the run in 1921. The CID had taken a statement from Mrs Flynn's son, the canon's nephew, about Ryans' movements on the night of Paddy Muldoon's murder. The canon's letter went on to say that Mac Eoin's assistance in securing any compensation that Ryans was entitled to would leave the curate 'free to leave at an early date'.[18]

Mac Eoin responded two days later telling the canon he would write to the army finance director that day and 'will hurry the matter as much as possible'.[19]

This correspondence was occurring some seven months after the general amnesty decision by the Free State authorities. Although Ryans was implicated in a still unsolved murder case, the opportunity to assist in him departing the jurisdiction at an 'early date' appears to have been very welcome to both clergy and the authorities.

Major General Mac Eoin's initial letter to his chief of staff, enclosing a copy of the canon's letter and setting out brief details of the compensation request, resulted in him receiving a communication requesting more information. Mac Eoin responded to his superior on 6 July, setting out the background to Ryans' arrest and the subsequent claim. He advised him of the details of the three military charges for which Ryans was arrested in Keadue at the end of March 1923 and told him that the car was seized at the same time.[20] Mac Eoin mentioned that Ryans was subsequently handed over to the civil authorities as he was wanted on a civil charge. Although Mac Eoin had subsequently given orders for the car to be returned to the Ryans family, before the order was carried out the car had been transferred to another army unit and stripped of many of its parts. The result was that after Ryans was freed from Mountjoy Prison in December 1923 he refused to accept the return of the car in its defective condition.[21]

There was no suggestion whatsoever by Mac Eoin, in either his response to Canon Donohoe or to his chief of staff, of any need either to check the status of the investigation into Paddy Muldoon's murder, or to acquaint the Civic Guard with Fr Ryans' intention to leave the jurisdiction. Yet it was less than five months since Rita Muldoon had pursued the case in the national newspapers and the department of justice had confirmed to Ambrose Lee that Dr Muldoon's case was still under consideration. Ryans had told Éamon de Valera over a year earlier that he thought Bishop Hoare and the State might be in league to effect his departure from the country. Developments were now proving that he was correct in his assumption and he himself may have decided to work the situation to his financial advantage.

However, it appears that the army's chief of staff wasn't solely relying on Mac Eoin for the full background to Ryans' compensation claim. On 3 July 1925, three days before Mac Eoin's response, Thomas Gorman, the army's finance officer, based in Griffith Barracks, Dublin, wrote to the attorney general's office. Gorman was seeking a legal opinion on the matter of Rev. E. Ryans and his claim for compensation for his Liberty Six motor car, taken from him by the army at the time of his arrest in March 1923. The letter outlines the facts of the case, the date when the car was seized and details about the car being dismantled and used for parts to repair army vehicles. It also stated that the army had previously refused Ryans compensation for his stripped car on account of the charges against him. Two of the charges, as detailed in Gorman's letter, are very similar to those outlined in Mac Eoin's letter to the army chief of staff making a case for Ryans to be compensated for the damage to his car. However, also included in the army finance officer's letter is an extraordinary fact about the arrest of Ryans two years before, one that is strangely missing from General Mac Eoin's letter of the same week:

> Father Ryans lodged a claim for compensation, and in the course of enquiries it was learnt from the Director of Intelligence that Father Ryans was interned for a time charged with–

> (a) Attempting to purchase from troops in Ballinamore a Machine Gun and Ammunition.

> (b) Holding up and threatening to shoot with a revolver a man named Rowley.

and extraordinarily:

> (c) Being an accessory to the Murder of Dr. Muldoon.[22]

Gorman says this information came to him from the 'Director of Intelligence'.

Mac Eoin's letter had also listed three charges against Ryans, as well as stating that his source was army intelligence, but made no mention of a charge of accessory to murder.

Maybe it was the fact that Mac Eoin was writing two years after the events of March 1923, but his omission of the charges connected to Paddy Muldoon's murder is strange to say the least.

On 8 July Thomas Gorman had his answer from the attorney general's office. The chief state solicitor's response made absolutely no reference to the three charges on which Ryans had been originally imprisoned in March 1923, possibly because the amnesty of the previous November covered any such acts committed in the Civil War, and the murder of Dr Muldoon would never have any hope of coming to trial. The opinion of the chief state solicitor was that the army had no answer to Ryans' compensation claim because the car was dismantled and used to supply parts to army vehicles:

> In those circumstances it would be impossible for the Army authorities to hand back the car to Fr. Ryans in the order in which it was when they took possession of it and in my opinion, Fr. Ryans would be entitled to get damages for the trover and conversion of his car.

The attorney general's officer then made an assessment that such damages:

> … would be, or might be assessed by a jury and in assessing such damages, regard would be had to the value of the car at the time it was taken possession of by Army authorities,

together with any loss which Father Ryans sustained by reason of being deprived of the use of the car.[23]

This legal opinion by the highest government legal office is made in spite of knowledge that the priest was 'interned for a time charged with being an accessory to the Murder of Doctor Muldoon'. The attorney general was the officer responsible for denying a bail application to Ryans when the issue arose after the first and second trials for the abandonment of the infant Rose Brown. Yet the same office that kept Ryans imprisoned while aggressively pursuing the child abandonment charges, was now of the opinion that the man charged in relation to Paddy Muldoon's murder should receive financial compensation from the State.

The processing of the priest's compensation claim moved fairly quickly. While Major General Mac Eoin was on holidays, one of his staff officers was able to write to Canon Donohoe, notifying him that Fr Ryans received £250 compensation on 25 July and 'is quite satisfied with the amount'.[24]

Ryans' satisfaction with the compensation was no doubt greatly exceeded by the sense of relief felt by the Free State authorities, the Catholic hierarchy and the IRA when he boarded the SS *Mauretania* on 24 October 1925, into exile.[25] Ryans was now experiencing the same fate as Cain in the Old Testament. Meanwhile, John Charles Keegan had already departed Ireland the previous month, landing in New York on 21 September 1925.[26] It seems incredible that Fr Ryans, a suspect for involvement in one unsolved murder, and Keegan, a connected suspect for this same murder as well as a number of similarly unsolved murders, were allowed leave the country, one with financial assistance from the State.

On the very day that Edward Ryans boarded the ship for America, Frank O'Beirne appeared before the Central Criminal Court in Dublin. However, the State was not pursuing his publicly admitted involvement in the IRA's investigation into Dr Muldoon's murder. He was instead found guilty of a more recent charge: 'being concerned in the organisation of a body purporting to be a military force, namely, the Irish Republican Army'.[27] He had been arrested some months earlier in possession of IRA documents (none of which would seem to have related to the IRA investigation into Dr Muldoon's death).

It is highly possible that the admissions made by Frank O'Beirne during the by-election earlier in the year about his continued involvement in the IRA, which Ambrose Lee brought to the attention of the department of justice, may have brought him under closer observation by the Civic Guards. O'Beirne was sentenced to twelve months in prison.[28]

Fr Ryans' departure would have come as a relief to both de Valera and Aiken, who had struggled unsuccessfully to deal with the controversy surrounding republican involvement in Paddy Muldoon's murder. However, his departure removed any remaining chance of Rita Muldoon obtaining justice for the death of her husband.

CHAPTER 17

Rita Muldoon continued to fight for every penny she felt she and her children were owed in the years after Paddy's death. It took until 28 April 1924, a full year after the murder, for the minister for finance to write to John A. Pettit with details of the decision of the Compensation (Personal) Injuries Committee in relation to the case of Dr Paddy Muldoon. In accordance with the committee's investigation and their report, the minister informed Rita's solicitor that an ex-gratia grant of £7,000 was payable in this case. This was just one-third of the amount claimed and, in addition, only £1,000 was to be paid to Rita herself in respect of her loss. The balance, £6,000, was to be lodged in court for the benefit of the children, who were minors.[1]

This was not a good outcome for the young widow and her children, as it meant that only £1,000 would be released directly to Rita. She would therefore be dependent on making applications on the children's behalf through the court system for many years to come, for funds to pay for their school fees, and later college fees, as well as other allowable expenditure.

It was not until another year had passed, in May 1925, that the compensation awarded to the Muldoon children was paid into the court system.[2] It is likely that the £1,000 payable to Rita Muldoon wasn't received until then either.

Rita also kept fighting on her dead husband's behalf. Her next public intervention was in connection with a more mundane matter, however. In October 1926, a year after Ryans had sailed for America, she brought a case at Longford District Court against Mr William Adair, a motor garage owner of Longford. This was the matter that Rita had been pursuing while recuperating in Dublin after the birth of her youngest child, Patrick Michael. It was stated in court that in 1921 Dr Muldoon had met with a motor accident and he later sold his damaged car to Adair, but it was never paid for. A judgment for £30 had later been obtained against William Adair in a Sinn Féin court, but he still hadn't paid. Adair had claimed an inability to pay the debt on financial grounds. The Longford District Court allowed the earlier Sinn Féin court ruling to stand.[3]

This was a rare victory for Rita in the immediate years after her husband's death. She had valiantly and publicly carried on the fight to uphold his good name and to obtain justice. In this difficult task, she received assistance from her brother Ambrose, though her in-laws, the Muldoons, did not seem to become involved in the struggle.

***

There was one young member of the Muldoon family, however, who could never forget the injustice done to his uncle. Thomas William Muldoon knew his dashing young uncle well from the visits he would make to the family farm in Cloodrumin, by motorbike or car. He was slightly fearful of his uncle's car, an uncommon sight at the time, and he was concerned that a wheel might run over his grandmother's foot as she often stood close to the car waving goodbye to her handsome son.[4] The circumstances of Paddy Muldoon's murder, and the failure of the authorities to pursue those guilty, would have a lasting effect on his young nephew.

As he grew up, Thomas William became obsessed by the injustice of the case and was to devote a great deal of his life to pursuing the perpetrators. Although he was poorly educated by comparison to his university-trained uncle, his dedication to his task was unfaltering to the point of obsession. His investigation into the events surrounding the murder was detailed and relentless. He sought out anyone he thought might assist him in obtaining the truth and justice.

Leitrim people by nature are somewhat reticent; 'pass no remarks' and 'no comment' are phrases often heard in an area that has learned to live and let live. Thomas William broke the mould in this regard, as he obsessively brought up the question of his uncle's contentious killing at every possible opportunity and spared nobody, including the Catholic Church and the authorities.

Nearly seventy years after his uncle's murder, Thomas William Muldoon gave a detailed interview outlining his lifelong quest to obtain justice, and revenge, for his family's loss. He also named his uncle's killer and his two accomplices.[5] In the interview, he recalled that a car was sent down to their house on the night of the shooting to collect his father, Frank. His father was brought up to Mohill to see the body of his young brother laid out with the fatal bullet wound that had severed one of the principal arteries in his neck.[6]

Thomas William later became familiar with the investigations of the CID into the events of the night of his uncle's murder. He knew the main suspect was Fr Edward Ryans, who drove the attackers, including their leader, John Charles Keegan, into Mohill that night.[7] Thomas William believed the other two members of the gang to be Cassels from outside of Mohill and Clyne from Ballinamore.[8] Joseph Clyne was the man found guilty, along with Keegan in November 1924, of having assaulted Civic Guards in Cloone.[9]

From his research, Thomas William was also aware that, some time after his uncle's killing, the anti-Treaty IRA had held an investigation into the death and had accepted responsibility, saying that Dr Muldoon had been shot by mistake. But he also believed that his Aunt Rita had answered a knock to her front door earlier on the night of her husband's death. The caller was seeking her husband to attend to a dying man, so she referred them to Canon Masterson's where Dr Muldoon was playing cards.[10] Yet no one called for him at the canon's residence that night. The only other alarm call for any local doctor that night, or the next morning, was to attend the mortally wounded Muldoon. This highly suspicious occurrence on the night of the murder is not referred to in

Rita Muldoon's short diary. Perhaps Thomas William learned about it directly from Rita.

Thomas William's belief was that his uncle had told his friend Canon Masterson about Ryans' involvement in the young housekeeper's pregnancy. Masterson in turn informed Bishop Hoare and it was the bishop's reaction, in suspending Ryans after the child abandonment incident, that was the first reason for Paddy Muldoon's murder. A second reason for his uncle's killing was the upcoming court case in Dublin against Fr Ryans and Kate Brown on the child abandonment charges.[11] It seemed Ryans was afraid of what the doctor would reveal when under oath.

Many years later Dr Muldoon's son Patrick (born after his father's death and himself a doctor) recalled what he was told by his mother about the events of the time. He said that Fr Ryans had approached his father and requested him to 'see to things' in respect of Mary Kate's condition.[12] Dr Muldoon refused to carry out the procedure, a termination of the pregnancy, and informed his acquaintance, Canon Masterson, that there was a local curate in trouble and he required all the help that could be given to him. Patrick's brother, Desmond, was also adamant that their father had been approached to perform a termination.[13] Their sister Olwyn informed her sons that her father's murder was arranged by Ryans to silence Paddy.[14] The situation had only become more desperate for the priest after the abandonment of baby Rose in Dublin. Being suspected of fathering the child was bad enough, but the revelation that a priest asked for an abortion? There would have been no recovering from that.

***

By 1933, the tenth anniversary of Paddy Muldoon's murder, Thomas William, still a teenager, had commenced his personal crusade to obtain justice. That year he approached Canon Masterson, who told Thomas William, 'We can't say whether Fr Ryans shot your uncle or not but through drink he got the girl in trouble.' Thomas William then asked him whether Ryans could continue as a priest after being the father of a child. The canon replied, 'Well if he confessed to the bishop and if the bishop gave him forgiveness he could be a priest again.'[15] How much more of the affair the canon and the doctor's nephew discussed is not recorded.

Some years later, when in his early twenties, Thomas William was still troubled by his uncle's killing. In the absence of any justice being obtained for the family loss, his thoughts turned to revenge and he often asked his father, 'Why didn't you shoot Fr Ryans?'[16]

Frank Muldoon was a religious man and he believed that there was a black sheep in every flock. He was a rural farmer and a practical man who didn't have the educational and career opportunities of his younger brother. Nor did he socialise with the professionals and clergy of the area, with whom Paddy Muldoon mixed so easily. Frank Muldoon saw no point in shooting Fr Ryans in revenge. He simply got on with his farming and generally avoided the subject of his brother's death.

Frank never talked much about what had happened, but Thomas William knew that whatever his father did say could be believed. Frank told his son one day that Paddy should never have had anything to do with Ryans. He recounted an incident that occurred when Fr Ryans made a crude and insulting remark in his brother's home on Fair Day in Mohill. That one meeting with Ryans was enough to convince Frank Muldoon that he was someone to be avoided.[17]

Thomas William's sense of injustice only grew after hearing this. After all, the killers of Dr Paddy Muldoon were never charged with the crime. Thomas William came to believe that Kevin O'Higgins, the Free State's first minister for justice, intervened to prevent the suspects being charged.[18] He said in his interview that O'Higgins had travelled down from Dublin to meet with Bishop Hoare. The bishop asked him to prevent a disgrace to the Catholic Church and to leave it to the Church to deal with Ryans.[19] Thomas William believed that as a result of this meeting a deferential State wound down the investigation to avoid an embarrassment for the Church. Both parties were later happy to get rid of Ryans to America. While it hasn't been possible to directly corroborate Thomas William's story, much of the rest of the information he provided has been verified by other sources. He seems to have been careful to avoid wild speculation.

***

When Fr Edward Ryans went to America in 1925, he initially assisted Dean Thomas Tubman in the parish of St Thomas Aquinas in Reno, Nevada. Fr Tubman was from Leitrim and was the original owner of the car that Ryans was seen driving on the night of Paddy Muldoon's murder.[20]

After a short stay in Reno, Fr Ryans moved to the parish of the Holy Redeemer in Kissimmee, Florida and served as pastor of that parish for a few years. In June 1928 he made a visit back to Ireland and England.[21] He made another return visit to Ireland in April 1936, which coincided with the Golden Jubilee celebrations for St Patrick's church in Mohill. Ahead of the celebrations, Canon Masterson had a bell tower and steeple added to the church, with a new sanctuary, altar rails and grand organ inside.[22] It would have been these new features that Ryans saw on his return.

However, it was not the Fr Ryans of old who turned up in Mohill for the Jubilee celebrations. Gone was the combative and confident personality whose career had so spiralled out of control on the streets of the same town some thirteen years earlier. Instead an older, very tearful and penitent Fr Ryans was once more looking for someone to intercede on his behalf. On this occasion he approached Canon Masterson, Dr Muldoon's old card-playing friend, who was busy supervising the Jubilee celebrations. Surprisingly, Masterson agreed to help.

On 15 April 1936, Canon Masterson wrote to Bishop James McNamee, who had replaced Bishop Hoare in the

Diocese of Ardagh and Clonmacnois after the latter's death in April 1927. He commenced his letter by stating, 'I have just had a visit from Fr Ryans.'[23] Without feeling any necessity to acquaint the new bishop of the background to the story, the canon said Ryans 'was looking very well and is very penitent'. He went on to say that he had 'long since abandoned any suspicions I once entertained about his complicity in the Muldoon case. He is completely free of that charge.'

The canon had underlined the word 'that' in 'that charge', inferring that Ryans' penitence related to the other charge, that of getting his young housekeeper pregnant. He continued that Ryans had 'besought me, with tears, to ask your Lordship to accord him an audience, however brief, on next Friday or Saturday'.

It is hard to imagine Edward Ryans in tears when we recall the belligerent and assured nature he exhibited all through his dealings with the previous bishop and with others. Whether he was genuinely penitent or just a good actor, it was clear that he had no desire to remain in exile in America, a wanderer like Cain in the Old Testament.

At Ryans' request Canon Masterson enclosed two documents with his letter to the bishop, and mentioned that his visitor knew that he could not hope for a place in Ireland. The canon's letter ends with a postscript, advising that Ryans was staying with Fr John Casey at Levamore, Legan, and that he would await the bishop's reply there.

The canon's letter to Bishop McNamee does not explain

why he had long abandoned his suspicions about Fr Ryans' complicity in Dr Muldoon's murder. After all, it was only three years since he told Thomas William Muldoon that he was unsure whether Ryans was involved in his uncle's death.[24] Neither does Canon Masterson's letter shed any light on the contents of the two documents he was forwarding to the bishop on Ryans' behalf.

Fr John Casey, with whom Ryans was staying, had been curate at Aughavas previous to him. He was another priest who had been very active in the independence movement. He had also been a friend of Seán Mac Eoin and was a concelebrant at Mac Eoin's wedding in June 1922 in Longford cathedral.[25] However, Fr Casey had taken the Free State side in the Civil War and had been badly wounded when ambushed by anti-Treaty forces.

Like Fr Ryans, Casey had also written seeking Major General Mac Eoin's assistance many years earlier, when he was submitting a compensation claim in May 1923 for injuries sustained in the attack by anti-Treaty forces. Mac Eoin obliged by writing to President Cosgrave on his behalf. He also wrote to Intelligence Command asking if they knew anything about Fr Casey's belief that they had captured anti-Treaty documents relating to the attack on him. Casey was seeking an authenticated copy of any such document to support his compensation claim.[26]

Now, many years later, the two former Aughavas curates and Civil War adversaries had time to talk about the past while Fr Ryans awaited Bishop McNamee's response to Canon Masterson's intercession on his behalf.

CHAPTER 18

John Charles Keegan, who like Fr Ryans had departed to America in late 1925, also considered returning home in 1936. In August of that year, he stated in the course of a pension application, 'I intend to try and save a few $ to go home to Ireland to live.'[1]

A year earlier Keegan had written directly to Éamon de Valera to query whether he was eligible for a pension under the Military Pensions Act of 1934. This was to be the first of a number of unsuccessful pension applications Keegan would make between 1935 and 1975.[2] By this stage de Valera had led Fianna Fáil, the political party he set up, to power in the 1932 general election, only six years after its foundation. The Fianna Fáil minority government had introduced the Military Pensions Act in 1934 to broaden the scope of previous military pension legislation to include members of the anti-Treaty forces.

Keegan was to write directly to de Valera on three occasions between March 1935 and July 1938, even referring to him as 'My Dear Friend' in the second letter, seeking his assistance with his pension application. In his third letter, Keegan told de Valera, 'I take the privilege of writing so much to you about same. Knowing the way you understand my case.' On each occasion de Valera's private secretary acknowledged

Keegan's letters and forwarded them to his counterpart in the department of defence. In spite of these letters, John Charles Keegan's pension application took seven years to process.

In the course of his pension application, important aspects of Keegan's activities in the years 1917 to 1925 were recounted. In one letter, dated 23 January 1938, Keegan stated that on escaping from the imprisonment and death sentence that followed his involvement in the Longford Barracks breakout, 'I met Seán O'Farrell who was Commandant[.] I was then Vice Commandant.'

Seán O'Farrell furnished a rather exaggerated reference to support Keegan's pension application, including a great number of incidents that Keegan himself did not claim, noticeably an ambush of British forces during the War of Independence period. However O'Farrell did state some things that appear grounded in fact, such as that during the Civil War, Keegan took part 'in two attacks on Mohill Barracks in March and April 1923', and Keegan himself claimed 'Two attacks on the Military Bks in Mohill'.

Bearing in mind that the IRA statement of May 1924 described the killing of Paddy Muldoon in March 1923 as an attack on a Free State patrol in Mohill that went wrong, O'Farrell and Keegan's pension submissions seem to confirm Keegan as being one of Muldoon's attackers.

Keegan had stated that his active service took place in Leitrim, Roscommon and Longford. It would seem that the brigade committee of the North Roscommon Brigade was ultimately appointed as the deciding referee for his claim, and it came back with the response that Keegan 'was not a person to whom the Act applies'.[3] Therefore, his claim was rejected. There was no explanation given for the assessment and it would not be until 1964 that Keegan would reapply for a military pension.

***

The outbreak of the Second World War saw many Irishmen volunteering to join the British Army, while the country itself remained neutral. The war also brought opportunities for men and women from the twenty-six counties to fill large manpower gaps in Britain caused by recruitment to the British Army and Royal Navy, in building, armaments factories, heavy industry and the health sector. Thomas William Muldoon was one of the people who took up this employment opportunity.

When Thomas William, then in his mid-twenties, went to England in 1941, he experienced the horror of the frequent air raids. By that stage he had abandoned his Catholic religion and all religious belief as a reaction to what he had discovered from his enquiries into his uncle's murder. He couldn't accept that God would have allowed a priest to arrange the killing.

Although he frequently returned to Ireland, Thomas William stayed working in England long after the war's end. He was employed on major building projects from Birmingham in the midlands up to Cumberland in the north. In 1950 or 1951 he met up with one of his cousins – Paddy Muldoon's oldest son, Llew. All three Muldoon sons had followed in their father's footsteps, graduating as doctors, and all three lived in England during the 1950s. Llew Muldoon had been a doctor with the British Eighth Army, which had fought in the desert campaigns in North Africa and seen action in Italy during the war.

Thomas William provided Llew with a copy of the newspaper report on Paddy's killing and subsequent inquest.[4] He told him everything he knew about the murder, how he knew beyond a shadow of a doubt that Fr Ryans was responsible. Llew listened, taking all this information in. Some time later, Thomas William came away from a late evening discussion with Llew with the understanding that, if he located Fr Ryans, his cousin would 'get him done in from someone of the Eighth Army'.[5]

Thomas William was still intent on revenge. And now, it seemed, he'd persuaded Paddy's eldest son to join him in his mission.

When he was next home in Ireland he made a point of arranging a meeting with Bishop McNamee, Bishop Hoare's successor, in Longford. It was at this meeting he discovered that Canon Masterson's intervention in 1936 had resulted in Fr Ryans getting a placement in England, the country where he was born. Thomas William didn't mention to the bishop that he himself was working in England, but he managed to obtain from him the information that Ryans was living in Lancaster, in the north of England. The bishop wasn't any more specific than that, but it was enough for Thomas William to go on.

One Sunday, after returning to England, Thomas William drove down to Lancaster from Cumberland, where he was working, to search for Fr Ryans. He attended many Masses without success, until, finally, an inquiry to a priest led to the information that Ryans was attached to St Mary's church in Lower Street, Morecambe, which was about five miles from Lancaster.

Thomas William had acquired a motorbike by this stage and for the next few Sundays, and even one Saturday, he would drive to Morecambe and attend the different Masses. He would speak to members of the congregation at the end of each Mass to obtain the name of the celebrant, but never heard the name Ryans mentioned. Finally, he attended Mass given by a priest he hadn't seen previously and when a lady dropped her glove, Thomas William retrieved it and took the opportunity to ask her the priest's name. 'That's Fr Ryans,' she informed him.

Thomas William approached the priest as he was leaving the church, with the excuse that he wanted a Mass said for his sick father in Ireland. He gave a false surname and, without telling the priest where he himself was from, he got Ryans to tell him that he was from Keadue. Thomas William gave the priest an offering of five shillings to say the Mass and Ryans said he would see him again the following Sunday, assuring him 'your father will be all right'.[6]

The Keadue home address given by the priest convinced Thomas William that he had found his man, so he got on his motorbike and drove straight down to Llew Muldoon in Staffordshire. He told his cousin that he had located Fr Ryans in Morecambe and had been talking to him earlier that very day. He asked Llew whether he was still prepared to have him 'done in' by someone from the Eighth Army. Llew's more sober response was, 'Now listen, if I get that done, that man might be arrested and I might be implicated, and two wrongs won't make a right.'

Thomas William then came up with another plan. He asked his cousin if he would accompany him to Morecambe the following Sunday, and go up on the pulpit while Ryans was celebrating Mass and say 'this man shot my father'. Thomas William said that he would identify Ryans to him and even walk up to the altar with him.

But Llew was not agreeable to this plan either. He told Thomas William that since he had last spoken to him, his mother, Rita, had met Fr Ryans by chance in a Dublin hotel. Ryans came over to her and enquired whether she still thought he was responsible for her husband's murder. When she said that if he was Fr Ryans she didn't want to talk to him, the priest walked off without any further words spoken.[7] Like his mother, Llew now wanted nothing to do with Ryans.

After all the work he had put in, Thomas William couldn't hide his annoyance with his cousin, whom, he felt, should have shared his desire to exact revenge on the man who had his father shot.

Thomas William firmly believed that family honour required either his own father or the sons of Paddy Muldoon to avenge the killing. He didn't think that he himself would get away with killing Ryans, as he had exposed himself in tracking him down. However, as he made his way back north to Cumberland the following Sunday afternoon, he stopped in Morecambe yet again, this time with a definite plan of action. He wasn't about to allow Ryans to get away scot-free.

He had obtained details of where Ryans lived from the lady who dropped her glove the previous week. Arriving at the house, he knocked on the door and was ushered in by the housekeeper, who went to let the priest know he had a visitor. When he was directed into another room Ryans was there and the priest immediately asked him if he had received bad news about his father. Thomas William replied that his father was dead a long time but he wanted a statement from the priest about 'another dead man in Mohill, Dr Muldoon'. He also told him that he had used the story about a sick parent to strike up a conversation to satisfy himself that he was the priest accused of the doctor's murder.

Fr Ryans calmly complimented his visitor on the courage he had shown in coming back to confront him. He then produced two documents that, he claimed, would prove his innocence of anything to do with the shooting. Thomas William recalled later that one was a letter from 'Seán O'Farrell, whatever title, he was in the IRA'.[8] O'Farrell was, as we have seen, John Charles Keegan's commandant after Keegan's defection from the National Army to the anti-Treaty IRA in November 1922. Seán Lemass had referred to O'Farrell as the 'IRA Brigade O/C' of Dr Muldoon's attackers in his July 1924 report to Frank Aiken, then chief of staff of the IRA. O'Farrell still had the title of OC, Leitrim IRA, when he resigned from the republican movement in 1934 to join Fianna Fáil. Like earlier IRA statements, O'Farrell's letter maintained that Paddy Muldoon was killed by mistake and that Ryans had nothing whatsoever to do with the shooting.

But the second letter was more shocking, in view of its source. Thomas William said in his interview that it was from 'Seán Mac Eoin, Minister for Justice of Eire'.[9] Ireland had become a republic in 1949 and Seán Mac Eoin served as minister for justice from February 1948 to March 1951. This letter also stated that Paddy Muldoon was shot by mistake.

Fr Ryans then told Thomas William that he had taken the two letters from Mac Eoin and O'Farrell to Bishop McNamee. It would seem that they were the two documents enclosed with Canon Masterson's letter to the bishop on Ryans' behalf in April 1936. If that were the case, though, the Mac Eoin document predated his period as minister for justice, so Thomas William must have been applying this title retrospectively. However, it was still a highly unusual document to have been issued by Mac Eoin, even if it was written previously in his capacity as a high-ranking army officer or TD.

After production of the two documents, Thomas William and Ryans argued about whether the shooting was accidental or not. The priest then claimed that, some time after the shooting, in Cloone, he met up with a brother of Dr Muldoon who said to him, 'Fr Ryans I know well you have nothing to do with my brother's shooting.' Thomas William told the priest that was a lie, but not being as well educated or erudite as Ryans, it was always unlikely that he would come away with any satisfaction from a verbal encounter with the priest.[10] He was also clearly thrown by the priest's production of the two letters. Still, he had certainly unsettled Ryans in his previously peaceful exile.

Not satisfied with the outcome of their meeting, Thomas William decided that his next intervention in Ryans' affairs would be far more direct and damaging. He knew he couldn't get his cousin Llew to denounce Fr Ryans publicly, so he proceeded to have a one-page account of the incident typed up for distribution in and around St Mary's church in Morecambe.[11] The leaflets were headed up:

THIS IS A TRUE HISTORICAL INCIDENT. WHY WAS DR M.P. MULDOON SHOT?[12]

The leaflets identified Fr Ryans by name and address, accused him of getting a girl pregnant, of seeking an illegal abortion, and of arranging for Dr Muldoon's murder ahead of the child abandonment trial. It stated that before the trial took place the priest had Dr Muldoon shot, as he was afraid the young doctor would make a statement 'as to who was the child's father'. The leaflet drew to its conclusion with a rebuttal of the IRA contention that the killing was a mistake by pointing to the fact that its men were locals who would have recognised the doctor and that he was shot after he was identified as being Dr Muldoon. The last sentence of the sheet touched on Thomas William's abiding reaction to the hypocrisy that, he considered, infected the Church: 'there can be no mistake that the tragic death of Dr Muldoon was instigated by the Rev. Father Ryan [*sic*], who still professes to save souls'. The leaflet was signed: 'By one who can never forget'.

Thomas William drove back to Morecambe and placed the leaflets in St Mary's church, and in the letterboxes on Lancaster Road, where Fr Ryans lived, with a generous handful placed in the priest's own letterbox.

The delivery of the leaflets must have come as a shock to Ryans and he would have been left in no doubt that the perpetrator was his recent visitor. Ryans' anonymous existence in the English seaside town had been well and truly shattered. The reasons behind the brutal murder of Paddy Muldoon in Mohill in 1923 were now being discussed among St Mary's parishioners and Ryans' neighbours.

The leaflet drop would also have been an embarrassment to the Catholic Church in Morecambe. Apparently it had the desired effect, as Thomas William reported that Fr Ryans 'was stopped saying Mass after that time'.[13] He was no longer saving souls.

***

Thomas William did not confine his attention to Edward Ryans; he also made it his business to track down and confront the suspects for the actual shooting.

Although not a tall man, Thomas William had a formidable appearance, having developed a strong physique after years of farm work and labouring on construction sites. He was indeed a tough individual, and not someone with whom you would want to get into a fight.

Cassels, one of the three implicated in the attack, had, like Keegan, gone to America. He returned to Leitrim in 1950 and Thomas William tracked him down and approached him one day near Mohill. He had spent years gathering information on his uncle's murder from every source he could. He had spoken to an IRA member who had attended the original IRA investigation and had told him that Cassels was the one who had called to the Muldoon house on the night of the murder seeking a doctor. Thomas William confronted Cassels and demanded of him, 'Did you shoot Dr Muldoon, were you at the shooting?'

Cassels answered, 'No I wasn't', and went on to claim that

he was in Roscommon and not in Leitrim at all on the night of the shooting.[14] Once again, Thomas William was forced to leave a confrontation with one of his uncle's killers with no answers and no satisfaction.

About four or five years after his meeting with Cassels, Thomas William learned, from the same IRA contact who was at the investigation, that Cassels was now in a home for the elderly in Kilmainham, Dublin. He visited Cassels in the home, where he was confined to his bed, and told him that he had received more information since their last meeting confirming his presence at the shooting of Dr Muldoon. According to Thomas William's recorded account, given to Leitrim County Library, Cassels responded, 'Well I never … I was standing over in the street from where Muldoon was shot and I saw John Charlie, we thought he was a Free State soldier, Keegan thought he was a Free State soldier. He put up the rifle and he shot him.' Cassels apparently denied that Edward Geelan, who was accompanying the doctor on the night, called out the doctor's name.

When Thomas William returned to Leitrim he reported Cassels' statement to the gardaí in Carrick-on-Shannon in an attempt to get his uncle's murder investigation reopened. He was told six months later by the superintendent dealing with the case that they could not get any satisfactory information from Cassels. Thomas William wasn't convinced that Cassels was ever actually questioned in Dublin by the gardaí.[15] Perhaps this attempt to have the case reopened in the mid-

1950s might account for the copy of the original 1923 police investigation being presently available.

Thomas William had also kept tabs on Ryans after the leaflet incident and was aware that by 1964 he was resident in an old people's home in Lancaster. Thomas William was actually in contact with a Dr O'Grady, who was from Cork and had spoken to Ryans in the old people's home. Fr Ryans wasn't wearing a collar at the time, and when he informed Dr O'Grady that he was a priest, the doctor told him that he should be in a Catholic institution, but Ryans replied he was all right there.[16] Perhaps the Church had finally washed their hands of him after the leaflet incident?

Fr Ryans died in Lancaster Moor Hospital on 4 February 1964, from coronary artery disease.[17] By remarkable timing, John Charles Keegan sailed back from America on 14 May 1964, after a period of thirty-eight years living there.[18] And so, with Ryans dead, Thomas William now turned his attentions to Keegan.

Through his investigations he had acquired both a visual image of Keegan and an impression of the type of person he was. He was aware that Keegan was considered an elusive character and had an unusual appearance. He had discovered that during the Civil War Keegan 'had caused a lot of shootings and a lot of trouble, he was an outlaw, a madman'.[19]

After Keegan's return from America, Thomas William tracked him down at a sports event, a boat race near Keegan's home outside Cloone. Thomas William approached him and said, 'I'm told you are John Charlie Keegan, the man that shot Dr Muldoon.' Keegan replied, 'I never shot Dr Muldoon. He was my doctor, he treated me for bronchitis', to which Thomas William replied, 'You treated him with a rifle.'

Some time after that encounter, possibly spooked by his confrontation with Thomas William, Keegan went to live in England, but Thomas William managed to track him down and arranged for 'a man to do him in'.[20] But the would-be assassin failed to turn up at the agreed meeting point in Birmingham and, as a result, the by then elderly Keegan escaped Thomas William's retribution.

***

Thomas William Muldoon retained a belligerent attitude to the Catholic Church all his life. As the years rolled on, he would work on a Sunday, sometimes getting an earth-moving machine in to do work alongside the tarred road. This habit of working on clearing drains or rebuilding his walls along the roadside on a Sunday was not always convenient for his Mass-going neighbours, of course, but it was what they grew to expect from him.

In late 1967 Thomas William's eagerness to challenge the Church brought a rather unexpected response. He had apparently taken offence at a speech made by Canon James O'Dea, the elderly parish priest of Clarinbridge in County Galway.

The occasion of the speech was the unveiling of a small

memorial along the quay in Galway city, at the spot where the body of Michael Walsh, a Sinn Féin councillor, was found in October 1920 after he had been abducted and murdered by British forces. Canon O'Dea, a native of Ballygannor, near Kilfenora in County Clare, had been a young curate in Galway at the time of the killing, having been ordained in Maynooth in July 1919. The Galway diocesan records indicate that Canon O'Dea had a photographic memory and could 'regale his friends with the minute details of historical characters and events'.

Thomas William wrote to the canon, taking issue with some of his reported speech at the unveiling of the memorial stone. His letter to the priest also included an account of Fr Ryans and the murder of his uncle. On 8 November 1967, Canon O'Dea responded with a thoughtful and very empathetic letter.[21] The canon recalled that he was in attendance when the body of Michael Walsh was brought back to the home of his pregnant widow and seven children in a handcart. This tragic scene was similar to that experienced by Rita Muldoon, also pregnant, and her young family, when her husband's remains were brought back to their house on that night in March 1923.

Canon O'Dea went on to graphically describe the results of a massive head wound to the body of Michael Walsh. He told Thomas William that he had misunderstood what he had said at the unveiling and that he 'did not advocate return to the guns but to a spirit of unity, so badly needed in this country where self-interest, greed for wealth & power are everywhere'.

The canon's letter recounted that his own family had suffered intimidation and persecution at the hands of those with a greed for wealth and power. Their persecution went on for four years; one night, when only his mother and an elderly servant were at home, their house was sprayed with gunshots. Cattle were stolen and on another occasion his mother suffered pellet wounds 'in her arm & my brother several in his face & neck'. The canon suggested that this constant intimidation aggravated his brother's tuberculosis and brought about his death at age twenty-nine. In the end the home where his family lived for 300 years was sold as his mother was unable to carry on, while one of the two ringleaders of the intimidation was still prominent in local politics.

Then the canon, with his remarkable memory, turned his attention to Thomas William's own situation and addressed the 'tragedy in your family'. He said, 'I knew Mrs. Muldoon & her sister Mrs. O'Malley well & I remember the horror of those who knew the circumstances of Dr Muldoon's death. Bad priests, no more than other bad people, should not destroy your Faith, which is independent of them, God will judge them in his mercy and understanding.'

This remarkable letter appears to have renewed Thomas William's faith in at least one member of the Catholic clergy. He retained the letter and seems to have personally elevated the elderly canon to the position of bishop before providing Leitrim County Library with a copy.

Thomas William Muldoon's lifelong quest to exact revenge for his uncle's killing ultimately failed. He was seventy-seven when he gave his detailed account to Evelyn Kelly of the Leitrim County Library in February 1993. Even at that stage of his life he said that he was still very bitter about the case. It would not be an exaggeration to say that he had been obsessed all his life with his uncle's murder and the failure of the authorities to bring the perpetrators to justice.

Thomas William never passed up an opportunity to discuss the case, particularly after he returned to the family farm in Cloodrumin after many years in England. He would visit his neighbours, the Leydens, regularly on a Sunday evening. Each and every Sunday the Leyden family would have to listen to him talk again about Paddy Muldoon's killing.[22] In his later years, Thomas William's cousin Desmond, who was Paddy Muldoon's second son, came to him and together they continued their joint research and investigations into the murder.

Towards the end of his life Thomas William felt that he had achieved nothing as a result of his dogged pursuit of his uncle's case. This was not altogether true, however, as he had carried out a much more thorough investigation than the Civic Guard or the CID ever had. He had personally confronted Ryans, Keegan and Cassels, three of the four main suspects. He had spoken with members of the clergy, including Canon Masterson and Bishop Hoare's successor, Bishop McNamee. He also discussed the case with men who had served in the IRA and had knowledge of the lethal attack on his uncle. He claimed to have spoken to the IRA quartermaster who armed the assailants on the night of the killing, and the IRA man who disarmed them on the occasion of their initial investigation.

Thomas William spoke to anyone he felt might advance his knowledge and understanding of the case. He was able to tell us that, many years after the dreadful murder, Ryans was in possession of letters from Mac Eoin and O'Farrell proclaiming his innocence that seemed to tie in with Canon Masterson's 1936 letter to Bishop McNamee.

As well as all this, Thomas William also left a tantalising account of a conversation he had with Dr Muldoon's widow, Rita, in 1950 when he met her in a shop. He didn't specify where the shop was; maybe it was in Galway, or possibly in Maggie Ellis' or Maggie's sister's shop in Mohill. Rita told her husband's nephew that she had a diary, and that she had been told that it contained enough information to bring a murder charge against Fr Ryans.[23]

Thomas William also left behind a full account of the exhaustive investigations he carried out, together with his findings, and enough valuable information to enable the investigation to be picked up again.

CHAPTER 19

While investigating and reconstructing the events that followed the murder of Paddy Muldoon, it has become evident that there was a campaign of collusion between the Church and the State, as well as a separate attempt at a cover-up by the anti-Treaty IRA. The aim in both cases was to prevent disclosure of the truth behind the doctor's murder.

Fr Ryans himself commented on the likelihood of collusion between the hierarchy and State to engineer his departure from Ireland.[1] He told de Valera that the authorities had written to Bishop Hoare to say they had released Ryans from prison on condition that he would leave the country and that the Church and the State 'may be in league to effect this'.

It is not difficult to see why those in power would want to prevent the truth behind this murder from coming to light. Take Bishop Hoare, for example. Despite his experience in the office, the bishop must have been horrified by the events that unfolded in his diocese in late 1922 and early 1923. During the War of Independence Bishop Hoare had the task of keeping a close eye on a number of priests of the diocese who had become heavily involved in the political movement for independence and, in some cases, in the military campaign. The Civil War had only brought increased lawlessness and danger to the countryside, and there was always the fear that individual priests would participate in this conflict.

Bishop Hoare had without doubt been informed that Fr Edward Ryans, who had been causing him concerns for years through his political involvement, had made his young housekeeper pregnant, prior to his relieving Ryans of his position as curate. The identity of his informant, whether Canon Masterson, Fr Dunne or some other source, is uncertain, but what is certain is that the information had the potential to ignite an embarrassing scandal for the Church. Any hope of completely suppressing this scandal had been thwarted when Ryans and his housekeeper were arrested in Dublin and charged with the abandonment of a child.

Just over a month later, the murder of Dr Paddy Muldoon in Mohill, a highly respected man and committed Catholic, was being linked to Ryans and his anti-Treaty associates. Just when matters couldn't be expected to get any worse, Fr Edward Dunne, the young curate of Fenagh and a friend of Ryans, died following a period of sustained alcohol abuse, possibly due to guilt over his unintended role in instigating Dr Muldoon's murder. Moreover, CID detectives investigating the Muldoon case had discovered that on the night of Paddy Muldoon's murder, Fr Ryans had driven off from the home of Mrs Flynn of Aughavas, herself a relative of the bishop with strong connections to the priesthood.[2] The bishop found himself facing a scandal of nightmarish proportions; the reputation of the Catholic Church in

Ireland, and his own legacy, would depend on how he dealt with it.

It appears that Bishop Hoare moved quickly once Fr Ryans had been arrested and charged with child abandonment. The diocese received a copy of the deposition relating to the charges and evidence against Ryans, although there is no record as to how this was obtained. After he was charged, the bishop came down personally to Aughavas and suspended Ryans from clerical duty.[3] If the bishop had hoped that Ryans would leave the area upon this suspension, however, he must have been infuriated when reports came back of Ryans' drunken and violent behaviour in Mohill in the following weeks.

The rumours at Dr Muldoon's funeral about Ryans' involvement in the murder would certainly have reached the bishop. The anonymous letter the bishop had received in September 1920, suggesting that Ryans' activities would result in serious consequences and even bloodshed, was suddenly proved to be prophetic.[4]

From this time onwards there was an organised series of actions taken to contain the growing scandal facing the Church. And although there is no evidence of direct involvement between Mac Eoin and Bishop Hoare in the case, a relationship clearly existed between them, as demonstrated by the willingness of Mac Eoin to allow the bishop to deal with what he considered Church matters. While it was Mac Eoin's suggestion to involve the CID in the investigation, after he had identified Ryans as being the driver of the car that brought Paddy Muldoon's killers into Mohill, it is highly unlikely, given their relationship, that Mac Eoin would have allowed an investigation involving the priest to proceed without at least warning Bishop Hoare of the situation.

Within two weeks of the CID becoming involved, Fr Ryans' young housekeeper, Mary Kate Gallogly, was arrested on the morning of her scheduled appearance at court in Dublin and bundled off to apparently illegal detention in Mac Eoin's Athlone headquarters. She was not transferred for her court appearance in Dublin, although Edward Ryans had been, and subsequently she was not charged with any other crime. The arrest took place at the home of a Catholic curate, near to where the fateful meeting of 17 January 1923 had taken place at the residence of Fr Deniston. With Dr Muldoon dead and Mary Kate in detention, there was no danger of Fr Ryans' account of not being the father of the abandoned child, Rose Brown, being questioned or challenged in an open court.

Furthermore, the decision by the state prosecutor not to pursue the case against the absent Mary Kate fits with a contention that events were being manipulated. Her absence from court prevented the full extent of the potential scandal emerging through her testimony. Even if it wasn't the intention of the CID and the ministry of home affairs to prevent her giving evidence, the outcome was that Mary Kate Gallogly didn't get to tell her side of the story in court. The scandal was being contained.

While Bishop Hoare was Ryans' religious superior, he wasn't a police investigator and couldn't be expected to pursue a murder charge against his curate himself. However, from very early on, the bishop was trying to manage the situation by publicly pushing the notion of atonement by the killer of Paddy Muldoon, rather than justice for the doctor's family. That was the clear message in his published May 1923 letter, which accompanied his donation to the national appeal held on behalf of Dr Muldoon's family. There was no suggestion in his letter that anybody with information or suspicions should contact the Civic Guard; instead, it was a case of leave it to the confessional and the sinner.

It is evident from the letter written to the bishop by the chaplain of Mountjoy Prison after the second inconclusive child abandonment trial in July 1923 that Bishop Hoare was attempting to intervene in the case in some fashion. The chaplain's final comment was a hope that the scandal might be removed or atoned for, a hope that the bishop definitely shared.[5]

The question of bail was a noticeable aspect of the abandonment case. Even the magistrate in the second abandonment trial considered refusal to allow bail in the circumstances harsh, while the State continued to pursue the case with unusual effort. The objection to bail, for a charge typically carrying a one-month prison term, only served one purpose: to keep Ryans out of the way while the murder investigation faltered.

Because the Free State's general amnesty did not come into force until November 1924, a proper investigation of Paddy Muldoon's murder would have produced charges and even a court case if it had been pursued. Ryans himself felt that he was being detained in Mountjoy with his bishop's 'consent'.[6] The continued imprisonment of Fr Ryans and the illegal detention of Mary Kate Gallogly were apparently being used to manipulate the outcome of a murder investigation and contain a scandal.

The failure of the Irish newspapers, other than *The Irish Times*, to report on Fr Edward Ryans' three trials also indicates a degree of suppression by the Catholic Church. The fact that the Protestant *Irish Times* reported on all three shows that this couldn't have been a result of direct State censorship, which did exist during the Civil War period.

This failure to publicise the case denied many readers the opportunity to familiarise themselves with important aspects of the potential reason behind the murder of Paddy Muldoon. Nor would they have learned of Mary Kate's failure to appear for her trial, her committal to an asylum and the death of her daughter Rose. It is mainly due to the reporting of the three cases in *The Irish Times* that we are aware of events which otherwise might have been lost from the public record. The report on the third trial and the revelation that the infant Rose had died, for example, allowed us to uncover the tragic end to her short life in St Patrick's Mother and Child home in Pelletstown. Had the trials been properly reported by the national papers and the Leitrim papers at the time, it is conceivable that more evidence could have emerged in relation to Fr Ryans' involvement in Paddy Muldoon's murder.

It would have required effort by the Catholic Church to influence the many newspapers that might have otherwise reported on the trials. Yet the Church had the necessary power and national reach to effect such an outcome, although it could be argued that it was simply an act of self-censorship by the papers which kept the story from appearing. Either way, the Church certainly managed to massively reduce the impact of the scandal.

Thomas William Muldoon had no doubt that there was collusion between the State and the Church. He names Kevin O'Higgins, the minister for home affairs at the time, and Bishop Hoare, as the architects of this collusion. His account of the bishop telling O'Higgins to prevent a disgrace for the Catholic religion and saying that he would deal with the problem himself has a certain ring of truth, as that is effectively what happened.[7] The available records of the Civic Guard and CID investigations into the case bear out the involvement of Kevin O'Higgins, a most senior government figure and a devout Catholic.[8]

The importance of the Catholic hierarchy's support for the Free State government during the Civil War would not have been lost on either Kevin O'Higgins or Seán Mac Eoin. During that period of bitter fratricidal strife and government-authorised executions, some of which were carried out under

Mac Eoin's direction in his Athlone headquarters, the Church maintained its unwavering support for the Free State government and the National Army's campaign. That level of support at such a delicate time would make it difficult to refuse a request from Bishop Hoare.

However, for all of Thomas William's focus on Kevin O'Higgins, it was Major General Mac Eoin who was at the centre of the collusion and cover-up on the government's side. His involvement in the Dr Muldoon case is evident from the outset, and all the more damning, given that he was friendly with the Muldoons prior to the incident; in December 1922 he sent a Christmas card to the home of Dr Muldoon, one of the medical officers

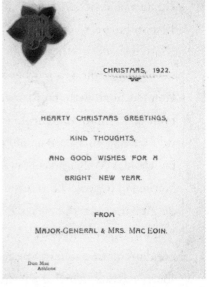

CHRISTMAS, 1922.

HEARTY CHRISTMAS GREETINGS,
KIND THOUGHTS,
AND GOOD WISHES FOR A
BRIGHT NEW YEAR.

FROM
MAJOR-GENERAL & MRS. MAC EOIN.

Dun Mac
Athlone

The Christmas card sent to Paddy and Rita Muldoon by Major General and Mrs Mac Eoin in 1922. (© The Muldoon/Donnelly family.)

to his Western Command. A few months later, however, he was going out of his way to assist Fr Edward Ryans, the man implicated in Dr Muldoon's murder.

Just four days before the actual murder, Mac Eoin was in Mohill inspecting the National Army barracks and discussing the military and policing demands that were facing his men there. It is probable that the armed and drunken activities of Fr Ryans in that town, less than two weeks earlier, came up in conversation during his visit. It would appear that even at this early stage Mac Eoin must have considered the curate's wild behaviour was something for Ryans' superior, Bishop Hoare, to deal with, a decision that was to have fatal consequences.

However, the reasons behind Mac Eoin's attitude in his later dealings with Fr Ryans are difficult to understand – even taking into account their friendship – unless the State was seeking to facilitate the Church hierarchy, as claimed by Thomas William Muldoon. It certainly seems that the National Army was turning a blind eye to Ryans' activities, despite the fact that Mac Eoin's own intelligence sources had information that Ryans was illegally carrying arms and even attempting to purchase a machine gun from Free State sources. Ryans felt free to carry arms 'with impunity', even accosting civilians with a revolver on the streets of Mohill, in spite of the presence of a National Army barracks in the town.[9] The fact that Ryans' behaviour in Mohill was brought to the attention of the military and yet they failed to arrest or disarm him raises serious questions about the level of protection he was receiving from within the National Army even before Dr Muldoon's murder.

Fr Ryans' eventual arrest didn't occur until after Mac Eoin's chance meeting with Rita Muldoon in Longford on

29 March. Even then, however, it was the charge of child abandonment that took precedence over any murder charge.

During the period of Ryans' detention, Mac Eoin met with him, was later in correspondence with him, and assisted him with various requests in spite of having already identified Ryans as being implicated in Paddy Muldoon's murder. It is worth mentioning again that Mary Kate Gallogly was arrested and prevented from appearing in court and giving evidence that might have provided a motive for Ryans' involvement in the murder. Her timely arrest, which bore the hallmarks of Mac Eoin's involvement, occurred after he received written pleas from his friend Edward Ryans. In addition, Ryans appears to have had no concerns about perjuring himself in the Dublin courts, although he had provided Mac Eoin with a written statement capable of undermining his own evidence. Mac Eoin kept a secret file for Fr Ryans when he should have been sharing any information he received with the murder investigation and the prosecution team in Dublin.

In June 1925, when Fr Ryans finally consented to leave the country, it was Mac Eoin who was approached by Canon Donohoe to arrange a compensation payment to help speed him on his way. When responding to a query from his chief of staff on the compensation claim, Mac Eoin never mentioned that Ryans, who was about to depart the country, was a suspect in the unsolved murder of Paddy Muldoon.[10]

One of the most questionable and unethical actions by Seán Mac Eoin during this whole scandal was yet to come.

This occurred when he took it upon himself to provide the exiled Fr Ryans with a signed letter stating that Dr Muldoon was shot by mistake. Mac Eoin had to be aware that Rita Muldoon had shown this to be an absolute falsehood, yet he was prepared to support his friend and continue the IRA charade.[11]

In 1929, having risen to the position of chief of staff, Mac Eoin resigned from the Irish Army. By April 1936, when Fr Ryans provided Canon Masterson with the two letters for Bishop McNamee, Mac Eoin was a Teachta Dála in the Dáil. He had no right and no authority to issue such a letter.

***

We are fortunate to have an almost complete insight into the IRA's attempts at collusion with Fr Edward Ryans and the suppression of the truth. The records of the IRA's investigation into Dr Muldoon's murder, and its subsequent reopening, have almost all survived, with the exception of any notes taken during the investigation's interviews of the attackers and the account John Charles Keegan provided directly to Éamon de Valera on his activities with the anti-Treaty forces.[12]

Frank O'Beirne's attitude to the crimes committed by members of the anti-Treaty IRA in the Civil War was public knowledge. While they had been called looters, robbers and murderers and were accused of being responsible for all the destruction, his attitude was that a state of war existed and as the anti-Treaty forces were not responsible for the war, they were not responsible for what followed.[13] It seems unlikely that someone of O'Beirne's views would ever oversee a thorough or objective investigation into Dr Muldoon's death. More likely, the investigation went through the motions, with its outcome of shielding Fr Ryans and the three attackers decided in advance.

As it transpired, O'Beirne even allowed Fr Ryans, technically the defendant in the investigation, the opportunity to vet a draft of the statement exonerating him.[14] However, both O'Beirne and Ryans were so impervious to the truth that neither of them seemed to take the trouble to examine the press reports on the inquest held into Paddy Muldoon's death, with fatal results for the accuracy of the subsequent IRA press release.

IRA Chief of Staff Frank Aiken's original position was that even if Ryans was guilty of being the father of Mary Kate Gallogly's child, the IRA should not allow him to be wrongly accused of the shooting of Dr Muldoon. Aiken still adhered to this approach even after he had received Seán Lemass' damning summary of Ryans' character and probable guilt.

In the immediate aftermath of the Civil War, much of Aiken's time was devoted to reviewing what had occurred during the hostilities and separating what the IRA considered to have been legitimate authorised actions from armed crime.[15] After Fr Ryans' direct plea to Éamon de Valera, president of Sinn Féin, in January 1925, Aiken undertook a new investigation into IRA involvement in the Muldoon killing. Two months later John Charles Keegan was moved to write to his old prison colleague, de Valera, complaining about the direction this inquiry was taking, and told him that he carried out orders 'to the letter'.[16]

De Valera undoubtedly took a direct involvement in the renewed investigation. Many years later, in his unsuccessful pension applications, Keegan said that he met de Valera after his release from prison and de Valera asked him to fill out a report on all his activities in the IRA. Keegan maintains that he filled out a report and 'delivered same personally to President De Valera'.[17] If he completed the report on his activities with the same misplaced bravado evident in the activity reports submitted with his later pension applications, de Valera would have been made fully aware of who ordered Paddy Muldoon's murder.

Whatever John Charles Keegan detailed in the report he gave to de Valera, other than Frank O'Beirne's election rally comments in February 1925, neither Sinn Féin nor the IRA came out publicly in Fr Ryans' defence after Aiken's renewed investigation. It had become clear that Paddy Muldoon's killing was not accidental, as they originally claimed, so the only avenue open to the IRA was either to state publicly who had ordered his shooting, or else to take Seán Lemass' advice and 'let the case drop'.[18] So the investigation was indeed dropped.

The subsequent July 1925 arms charge against Fr Ryans appears to have proved very useful to both Church and State. If there had indeed been an understanding between them to rid themselves of Fr Ryans, then Bishop Hoare stuck to his side of the arrangement. By refusing to appoint Ryans to any other position after his suspension from the Aughavas curacy in February 1923, the bishop effectively forced Ryans into exile in America. Although it was somewhat delayed, perhaps out of stubbornness, Edward Ryans finally succumbed to the 'Cain option'. Once he had left Ireland, there was little chance that he could ever be brought before the courts to face charges in respect of Dr Muldoon's murder, even on a private charge by the doctor's widow. Apart from a few short visits, Ryans would spend the rest of his life in exile.

The collusion between Church and State had succeeded, as the extent of the potential scandal to the Church had been greatly diminished. The Church's success in this regard had been heavily dependent on assistance from the State and much of the newspaper media. The amateurish attempts by the anti-Treaty IRA to cast doubt on the motive behind Paddy Muldoon's murder were of some assistance, too, for instance with unthinking republicans who would have accepted the organisation's version of events regardless of Rita's response. Together, the powers-that-be had managed to defuse a potentially enormous scandal and denied the Muldoon family any chance of seeing the doctor's killers brought to justice.

&PILOGUE

The murder of a loved one often brings lifelong suffering to their immediate family and can leave a legacy of injustice and loss to future generations. Nobody ever faced trial for the death of Dr Michael Patrick (Paddy) Muldoon; neither Fr Edward Ryans nor any of the attackers were brought to justice for his murder.

Likewise, there is no record of any charges being brought in respect of the string of murders and assaults on civilians in the same locality in the months following the killing of Paddy Muldoon. Nobody was charged for the deaths of Michael Reynolds of Clooneagh or Patrick Neville of Currycramp. No charges were ever brought for the attack on the McGuire family of Gubbs which left three of them with gunshot wounds, or for the murder of James O'Brien near Gowel in February 1924, nine months after the end of the Civil War. The killing of Free State soldier Edward Fitzgerald in Duignan's Pub in Ballinamuck was never prosecuted.

It seems that there was little appetite to follow up unsolved murders and aggravated assaults after the conclusion of the Civil War. It wasn't only those on the anti-Treaty side who had carried out criminally motivated actions; members of the National Army had also been involved in murders and other unlawful activity. In the aftermath of the bitter conflict the government was faced with the challenge of meeting the cost of the destruction of property and repairing the damage to the economy. There was little desire to properly investigate and pursue the perpetrators of the many crimes committed during the war. Newspaper reports for late 1923 and all of 1924 show only a small number of murder cases relating to the Civil War being prosecuted by the authorities in that period.[1] The introduction of the general amnesty in November 1924, a year and a half after the end of the war, effectively ended any hope of justice for many aggrieved families.

In addition to her grief, the upset of her children and the inevitable financial problems facing a young widow, Rita Muldoon had the added burden of publicly contradicting the anti-Treaty narrative of her husband's death. Rita's devotion to her husband's memory was evident in her response to republican announcements about the events surrounding his death. With some assistance from her brother Ambrose, she met what would have been an intimidating task with bravery and fortitude.

It is noticeable that Rita received no public assistance from the authorities in her struggle with the republican movement, and her personal papers contain no letters of support from Church or State. That Major General Mac Eoin was quick to intercede on behalf of others is evidenced by his efforts on behalf of Fr Ryans, and is also borne out in various cases that appear in his own archives as well as in some military pension applications for the period.[2] Curiously, he did not feel moved to come to the assistance of the widow of one of his medical officers with any of the information to which he had access.

Rita would be affected by the actions of Church and State in different ways at later stages in her life. She placed annual memorial notices in the national press. These can be found in the newspaper archives until 1936, the thirteenth anniversary of Paddy's death, when, as usual, there were two inserted, one in her own name and one on behalf of her children.[3] Both inserts refer to Dr M. P. Muldoon 'who was shot at Mohill. Co. Leitrim' on 18 March 1923.

This annual reminder of a family's grief appears to have become too much for at least one Catholic clergyman. Rita was called in by this clergyman, either a local priest in the Clifden area, or possibly even the bishop of Galway at the time, who told her to stop putting the memorial notices in the papers as it 'opened too many wounds'.[4] This was a particularly unchristian attitude, but Rita went along with the request, as there is no record of further memorial notices after 1936. She may have become worn down by events at this stage, and with three of her children attending Catholic schools in Ireland, she may have felt the need to protect them from any backlash.

The mean-spirited actions of the State had also been imposed on the Muldoon family a couple of years prior to this, in 1934, when Rita was obliged to move her two youngest sons, Desmond and Patrick, and her daughter, Olwyn, from the boarding schools they had been attending in England to schools in Ireland. It appears that political influence was brought to bear on the court's administration of the Muldoon children's compensation funds and their school fees for English schools or universities were no longer sanctioned.[5] Llewellyn, the oldest, came back to university in Dublin, while Desmond and Patrick commenced in Clongowes College in 1934. Olwyn attended the Loreto Abbey in Rathfarnham; however, her fondest school memories were of the boarding school in Farnborough that she was forced to leave.

When they were not attending boarding school, Rita brought up her four children in her modest home in Clifden, from where they enjoyed roaming the countryside and playing on the beaches out towards Ballyconneely.

Her three sons all qualified as doctors and each graduation must have brought bittersweet memories for Rita. The three brothers ended up in practice in England where Patrick, the youngest, joined his uncle Alfred Lee in general practice in Hednesford, in the north of England. As previously mentioned, Llew served with the Eighth Army during the Second World War, while Desmond emigrated to Calgary in Canada in 1953. Rita's daughter Olwyn also studied to be a doctor, but, like her mother before her, she gave up her medical studies to get married. She married an RAF officer, John Donnelly, in Belfast in July 1944, just a month after the Allied invasion of Normandy.[6]

Rita Muldoon and her husband's nephew, Thomas William Muldoon, maintained their separate struggles to uphold the memory of Paddy Muldoon and to achieve some form of justice for him. We have only one account of them meeting, in a shop in 1950. Thomas William came away from the meeting having been told by Rita that she had a diary that contained vital information. He later recalled how she had said that Justice Wyse-Power told her the diary contained enough information to bring a charge of murder against Ryans. Thomas William wasn't sure who Justice Wyse-Power was but thought the name was familiar.

Charles Wyse-Power was a judge of the Galway Circuit Court from 1925 to 1948. In that capacity he dealt with the applications for payment of school fees for Rita Muldoon's two younger sons in the late 1930s.[7] Desmond and Patrick were still minors and so the compensation payments they received in April 1924, in respect of their father's murder, were still under the control of the courts. It would seem that nearly fifteen years after her husband's death, Rita Muldoon had not given up hope of obtaining justice. She had availed of her dealings with a sympathetic member of the judiciary to discuss the prospect of a court case against Edward Ryans. However, Ryans was outside the jurisdiction, living in England at the time.

Many years later, in February 1997, Desmond Muldoon, the doctor's second oldest son, while writing to his cousin Thomas William, told him: 'The medical records that daddy kept are not available – perhaps misplaced.'[8] It would seem that Thomas William had not forgotten his 1950 meeting with

Rita, who had died in 1953, and had sent Desmond searching for his father's medical diary. He and Desmond put considerable effort into researching the doctor's murder at the time and were considering a book on the subject. Desmond wrote at one stage, saying that they 'might discuss the writer of the story later as we have more research to do in the meantime'.[9]

Desmond was aware that there was a possibility that his sister, Olwyn, might be in possession of documents belonging to his parents, but at this stage Olwyn was too ill to be approached.

It was discovered, years later, that Olwyn did have her mother's personal papers, and among them was the four-page, unsigned deposition written by Rita detailing the remarkable and shocking events that occurred between 17 January and 29 March 1923 in Mohill and the area surrounding it.[10] A deposition or testimony can include the setting down of an account of events that might be used at a later date in a trial. It is possible that Rita Muldoon's brother Ambrose, the Clifden-based solicitor, encouraged her to write out this account covering the events that led up to her husband's murder and the immediate aftermath. The 'diary', in the form of an unsigned deposition, which she had told Thomas William about in 1950, had finally been located.

**

As previously mentioned, after returning from exile in America, Fr Ryans ended up in Morecambe in Lancashire,

England. His younger brother, Vincent, also ended up living in Lancashire, in what is now the city of Preston.[11] In fact, all the Ryans family appear to have left Knockranny House in Keadue sometime after the Civil War.

Edward Ryans' sister, Margaret McKeon, left an account of the reason for their departure. Margaret had been a particularly active member of Cumann na mBan and managed to supply the IRA with explosives and detonators from the stocks in the two mines her father managed, while adjusting the books to conceal this fact. She continued to do so during the Civil War, supplying the anti-Treaty Arigna column. It seems the family came under suspicion, and the Free State authorities finally halted the supply of explosives to the mines Margaret's father managed. This resulted in the closure of the two mines and the loss of both Margaret and her father's livelihoods. Margaret was forced to go to England to seek employment and to set up a home there for herself and her parents.[12]

Thomas William Muldoon, of course, eventually caught up with Edward Ryans in Morecambe. Yet, despite the scandal and commotion that must have been caused by his leaflet campaign, the Catholic Diocese of Lancaster claims to have no record of Fr Edward Ryans or his attachment to St Mary's in Morecambe. Neither could they confirm any Church connection to the Morecambe address at which Ryans was living. It would appear that the priest, who on his own account had played his part in the struggle for Irish freedom, a part that so occupied Bishop Hoare's attention, didn't merit even a footnote in his adopted diocese.

In addition to this absence from the records of the diocese, Edward Ryans is also noticeably absent from his sister Margaret's detailed account of her War of Independence and Civil War activities. While she named her brother Vincent and Seán O'Farrell as referees for her activities, Margaret makes absolutely no reference to her brother the priest, who at different times was president of the South Longford and South Leitrim Sinn Féin Clubs. Neither does she mention the Longford Barracks escapees he drove to their Keadue home. In detailing the losses she and her family sustained on account of their support for the republican movement, she does not attempt to suggest that her brother's dismissal from his Aughavas curacy or his forced exile were in any way caused by his political stance.

Margaret returned to live in Ireland and died in 1976, thirteen years after the death of her brother Edward in England. In her will, dated 2 May 1973, she left the sum of £50 to Fr Young of Ballinamore for Masses to be said for the repose of the souls of her late husband, her brother Vincent and herself. Yet again there was no mention of her brother Edward, the Ryans family's black sheep.[13]

After all the excitement and danger of his life in Longford and Leitrim during the revolutionary period, Fr Edward Ryans lived out the last decades of his life in obscurity in England. Like many participants in the independence movement he would have looked back at the camaraderie and exhilaration of those heady days with the disillusionment of middle age. In Ryans' case there was also the guilt of his involvement in the deaths of Paddy Muldoon and Fr Edward Dunne, as well as his treatment of Mary Kate Gallogly and the death of her – and likely their – child. There is no record of him applying for medals or a pension in respect of his War of Independence and Civil War activities. When Ryans lay dying in Lancaster Moor Hospital in February 1964, he was without any of the trappings of his clerical or revolutionary past.

***

And then there is John Charles Keegan. After all the years spent in America, the timing of his return was remarkably close to the death in England of Edward Ryans. Shortly after his return, Keegan reapplied for a military service pension in July 1964.[14] He had previously been turned down for a pension award in May 1942. In his renewed application he claimed to have met his former prison colleague, Éamon de Valera, three times while in America.

After his return to Ireland, Keegan managed to arrange a meeting with de Valera, who was by then president of Ireland. The president found the time to give him some advice about his pension application, telling Keegan that his case was 'different'. Keegan was to spend a further eleven years unsuccessfully pursuing a pension or special allowance, before being finally turned down on the basis of his existing income in October 1975.

In pursuing his application from 1964 to 1975, he added to the account of his involvement in the War of Independence and the Civil War that he had provided in support of his earlier failed application. Keegan's account of his activities has an unusual quality when compared to other pension applications. He exhibits no recognition or sense of regret for the disastrous and divisive Civil War. He lists off his attacks on various National Army barracks and the unarmed Civic Guard, as well as his shooting of a soldier in Ballinamuck, with a misplaced bravado. He makes no reference to the murderous attacks on civilians during the latter stages of that war with which National Army intelligence reports associated him and his gang.

Many of the attacks that were ascribed to Keegan's gang during the Civil War bear a similar pattern: reckless and violent night-time attacks on rural family homes in pursuit of a single individual. The setting for the murder of Paddy Muldoon was different, but like nearly all the gang's targets, he was unarmed.

Whatever the driving force behind Keegan's activities in the latter part of the Civil War, it is evident from his own account and National Army intelligence reports that he needed little reason for violence. He had become someone quite capable of shooting an unarmed civilian and doctor, even one who had treated him for bronchitis. Edward Ryans would certainly not have found it difficult to persuade someone like Keegan to carry out the murder of Paddy Muldoon.

Remarkably, despite all the intelligence the National Army held on him, following his capture Keegan only ever faced a charge of assaulting three Civic Guards in Cloone. However, in the poisoned and fearful atmosphere after the end of the Civil War, it may have proved impossible to get ordinary civilians to give evidence against Keegan and his gang.

Seán O'Farrell, Keegan's commandant, later provided him with a reference stating that Keegan took part in more than 130 different operations, yet very few pension applications by other South Leitrim War of Independence or Civil War veterans make any mention of John Charles Keegan. His and Fr Ryans' one-time colleagues and comrades in general have opted to claim no part in any of their activities; they have effectively been deleted from the narrative of those years.

In the 1960s, after Keegan's return from America, an Old IRA march taking place in Mohill was held up for half an hour as participants objected to Keegan's participation.[15] Towards the end of his struggle to claim a military pension he was living in England with his nephew, and he died in a Leeds Hospital in May 1977.[16]

***

The shooting of Paddy Muldoon was one of many appalling acts of violence in a Civil War that became marked by such brutality in its latter stages. The month in which he was murdered, March 1923, became infamous for the atrocities carried out by both sides, but particularly by the National Army.

It would seem that the spate of murderous attacks on civilians in South Leitrim was in some way a response, by an out-of-control element on the anti-Treaty side in the locality, to the government's policy of executing anti-Treaty prisoners. Fr Edward Ryans was able to use this poisonous atmosphere to convince some of his anti-Treaty comrades, led by a pro-Treaty defector, that an innocent local doctor was a legitimate target.

What is unique about the Muldoon case is the number of national figures who became embroiled in the contentious and murky aftermath. De Valera, Aiken and Lemass on the anti-Treaty side and O'Higgins, Mulcahy and Mac Eoin on the government side. All of these figures went on to have long and successful careers in Irish politics, with the exception of Kevin O'Higgins, minister for justice. O'Higgins died in July 1927, at the age of thirty-five, as a result of gunshot wounds inflicted by republicans, partly in revenge for his prominent part in the government's Civil War execution policy.[17]

Having risen to the position of chief of staff, Seán Mac Eoin retired from the army in 1929 in order to follow a career in politics. In his long political career, he served as minister for justice and later minister for defence, and was an unsuccessful candidate for the Irish presidency in 1945 and 1959, before finally retiring from politics in 1965.

Richard Mulcahy resigned from the position of minister for defence in March 1924 but attained ministerial position again in 1927. He succeeded William T. Cosgrave as leader of Fine Gael in 1944 and served as minister for education and minister for the Gaeltacht on different occasions, before retiring in 1961.

Frank Aiken, the one-time IRA chief of staff, and his intelligence officer, Seán Lemass, were both closely involved with the founding of Fianna Fáil in 1926, endorsing de Valera's decision to drop abstentionism and take the constitutional route to further republican aims. Aiken had been elected a member of the Dáil in 1923, and in a fifty-year political career he held many ministerial positions in Fianna Fáil governments, serving as Tanaiste from 1965 to 1969, before retiring in 1973.

Seán Lemass was arguably the only individual from the anti-Treaty or pro-Treaty camps who came out of the Dr Muldoon affair with any credit. He carried out his investigation as best he could and his report was clear and forthright, while his assessment of the character of Fr Ryans was withering. He identified him as being the father of 'Kate Brown's' child and a definite suspect in the murder of Paddy Muldoon. However, his suggestion to Aiken that they allow the whole matter to drop was designed to limit the damage caused by the earlier IRA press statement and it offered no assistance to Rita Muldoon and her family in achieving deserved justice. He did at least infer in his report that Rita might be interviewed as part of the IRA investigations.

Lemass also went on to have a long and successful career in politics, holding many ministerial positions before succeeding Éamon de Valera as Taoiseach in 1959. After turning his back on his earlier commitment to protectionism, Lemass was widely regarded as one of Ireland's finest Taoisigh. He resigned from that position in 1966 and retired from politics in 1969.

How often any of those involved in the aftermath of Paddy Muldoon's murder had reason to remember the case during their long careers in national politics is not known, although we are aware that Seán Mac Eoin continued his highly questionable involvement by providing Fr Ryans with a document, in the nature of a letter of comfort, clearing him of any involvement in the Muldoon murder.

However, in the case of Éamon de Valera, who was the most successful post-Civil War figure, we do know that John Charles Keegan, his old prison colleague, had a habit of contacting him and no doubt reminding him of the dreadful fratricidal conflict. De Valera's championing of the anti-Treaty cause had given it a credibility and a momentum it otherwise would not have had, resulting in a more prolonged and destructive conflict than might otherwise have occurred. After the military defeat of the anti-Treaty cause, he belatedly came around to the constitutional path of gradually working towards a republic, and in doing so confirmed Michael Collins' much earlier espousal of a stepping-stone route to that ultimate objective.

In 1933 the oath of allegiance, the mainstay of the bitter Civil War, was abolished by de Valera's Fianna Fáil government, just ten years after the end of the conflict, without much objection from the British government. In 1949 the twenty-six counties were declared a republic by a Fine Gael government, the political descendants of Michael Collins and the pro-Treaty side. De Valera's hugely contentious pre-Civil War prediction, that Irishmen would have 'to march over the dead bodies of their own brothers' and 'wade through Irish blood' to achieve freedom, had been proved unfounded.

However, John Charles Keegan was one convert to the anti-Treaty cause who had taken this prophecy literally. De Valera must have been fully aware of Keegan's and Ryans' involvement in the murder of Paddy Muldoon from his access to the IRA documents relating to their 1923 and 1925 internal investigations into the incident. In addition, as we have seen, Keegan had personally provided de Valera with a written record of his Civil War activities, and, in his later applications, stated that he had met him on three occasions while he was living in America. President de Valera afforded him an hour's meeting in Dublin on 25 August 1965, presumably at Áras an Uachtaráin, the president's official residence. Four years later, on 19 December 1969, Keegan was again writing to de Valera seeking an interview with regard to his pension application, having apparently called out to Áras an Uachtaráin the previous week in an unsuccessful attempt to meet the president.[18]

It would seem that throughout Éamon de Valera's long and distinguished political career, John Charles Keegan would periodically turn up to remind him of his debt and connection to a gunman, and prison colleague, from the country's most bitter and divisive period. Whether these meetings served to remind de Valera of his own part in the Civil War conflict and its many unnecessary deaths, including civilians such as Paddy Muldoon and the other South Leitrim victims, is not known.

***

Mary Kate Gallogly appears to have recovered from the trauma she suffered in her teenage years following her unplanned pregnancy. Her family have always believed her pregnancy was caused by Fr Edward Ryans. Although she had suffered a great deal from the conception to the loss of her baby Rose, which was followed by her unjustified arrest and later committal to an asylum, she had youth on her side and seems to have eventually recovered from the nightmares she was beset with in the Ladies Detention Camp in Athlone during May 1923.

The records show that she married a local man in 1933 and that they had a child in 1940.[19] Mary Kate may have been widowed subsequently, however, as accounts suggest that she emigrated to Lowell, Massachusetts, where she apparently married a man of Italian extraction.[20] The move to America would have allowed her a deserved new life, much removed from the tragic events of her teenage years. However, there is little doubt that Mary Kate would always remember her little daughter Rose and that awful damp February night in Dublin when she was being pressurised to hand her into care.

***

Kevin O'Higgins once said that 'the Catholic Church has not the courage of its convictions – never had'.[21] He was speaking in August 1918 and remarking on the disappointment of many Sinn Féin members at the Catholic Church's failure to provide formal endorsement to the independence movement.

O'Higgins' summation of the Catholic Church is borne out in the Church's response to the many scandals that would beset it in the decades that followed. The Church was given a position of power and influence in the newly independent Ireland by the government, with control of many services relating to children, unmarried mothers and other vulnerable individuals. When potentially damaging scandals arose in areas under its control, however, the Church's immediate derogation from basic Christian values, as it circled the wagons to protect its reputation and power, would become a constant pattern. The Church's failure to properly respond to the dreadful loss suffered by Rita Muldoon and her family was one of its first failures of conviction after the formation of the new state. But it would not be its last.

Although Rita Muldoon was only twenty-six when her husband was killed, she never remarried. She provided for her young family while at the same time publicly defending her beloved husband's memory. During her long, lonely days in her Clifden home, when her children were in boarding school or university, or, later, following their careers and life away from home, Rita would have had too much time to reflect on the past. She never managed to obtain the justice she deeply craved, although she retained the 'diary', with supporting documents and her husband's bloodstained shirt, all her life. Rita was wonderfully brave, but it is not surprising that the memory of the tragedy and the pain of the early months of 1923 finally became a burden too difficult to bear.[22]

Whenever the children asked her about their father, Rita would start to cry; in the end, they learned not to ask too many questions. Her son Des would recall that his mother was always singing the song 'Roses of Picardy', which had become popular many years earlier during the First World War, around the time Paddy and she first met and fell in love.[23] Des could particularly remember his mother singing the lines:

> but there's one rose that dies not in Picardy,
> 'tis the rose that I keep in my heart.

&NDNOTES

Prologue

1   Muldoon/Donnelly family records: Rita Muldoon personal account. Rita Muldoon wrote what appears to be a contemporaneous four-page account of events from 17 January to 29 March 1923, which she retained along with other documents relating to her deceased husband and other events that unfolded after his death.

2   *Ibid.*

Chapter 1

1   Muldoon/Donnelly family records: grandchildren (from interviews with, and private documents received from, the grandchildren of Paddy and Rita Muldoon).

2   *The Leitrim Advertiser*, 26 January 1922.

3   National Archives, Tithe Applotment Books 1833, http://tithe applotmentbooks.nationalarchives.ie/search/tab/home.jsp.

4   Muldoon/Faulkner family records (from interviews with, and private documents received from David Faulkner, Muldoon family relation). Like many Irish tenant farmers, the Muldoons bought out their holding under one of the Irish land acts passed in Westminster to reform land ownership in Ireland.

5   Muldoon/Donnelly family records: grandchildren.

6   *Ibid.*

7   *Ibid.*

8   Muldoon/Donnelly family records: Rita Muldoon personal papers, letter of reference dated 6 March 1918, from Dr Howell Evans of The Laurels, Blackwood, Monmouthshire describing his practice and the 'very high opinion I have formed of Dr

Muldoon's professional abilities and his exemplary conduct and irreproachable character'. He also described Dr Muldoon 'as a man of fine physique, enjoys excellent health and is capable of doing hard work'.

9   England & Wales, Civil Registration Death Index, Patrick Bernard L. Muldoon, August 1989, Newcastle Under Lyme, Staffordshire, Vol. 30, p. 840.

10 *Leitrim Observer*, 13 February 1954. In March 1918 the war was at a critical stage with the commencement of concerted German offensives along the Western Front resulting in heavy casualties. The ill-judged threat of the extension of conscription to Ireland by the British government in April 1918 was met by intense opposition from all elements of nationalism.

11 Over the course of three years, the Spanish flu pandemic – an unusually virulent strain of the virus – killed more than fifty million people across the world.

12 *Leitrim Observer*, 13 February 1954.

13 *Longford Leader*, 24 March 1923.

14 Muldoon/Donnelly family records: Rita Muldoon personal papers, letter branded 18 January 1923 from the Deputy Director General, Army Medical Services, 88 Merrion Square, introducing the 'bearer Mrs Muldoon' to the Paymaster General, Portobello Barracks 'in connection with the a/c of Dr. Muldoon for professional attendance on our troops'.

15 Muldoon/Donnelly family records: grandchildren.

Chapter 2

1   The railway provided a local service from Dromod, the main line station five miles to the south, through Mohill and on to Ballinamore and Belturbet, with a branch line to Arigna. The service closed in 1959 having catered for passenger travel and the transport of livestock to and from local fairs for more than seventy years.

2   Turlough Carolan, the famous seventeenth-century blind harpist, lived in Mohill for many years and there is a statue erected in his honour at the bridge just opposite St Mary's Church of Ireland church, which is reputed to have been built on the site of Saint Manachán's monastery.

3   Kerr/Courtney family account.

4   *Longford Leader*, 14 October 1905.

5   Ardagh & Clonmacnois Diocesan Records, Biographical. Diocesan material mainly consists of correspondence between Fr Edward Ryans and Bishop Hoare, other correspondence relating to Fr Ryans, and some biographical details relating to Fr Ryans and other diocesan clergy. It also contains a copy of the City Sessions Court Deposition of 14 February 1923, relating to the charge of child abandonment against Fr Ryans and Kate Brown (Mary Kate Gallogly).

6   Corr, Elizabeth,'Up Longford', *Teathbha: Journal of County Longford Historical Society*, Vol. IV, No. 3, 2016, pp. 259–66.

7   Ardagh & Clonmacnois Diocesan Records, letter dated 17 January, Fr Ryans to Bishop Hoare.

8   The Roscommon by-election earlier in 1917 saw Count George Plunkett elected with the support of Sinn Féin. Fr Michael O'Flanagan of Roscommon was heavily involved in Plunkett's election campaign.

9   The victory for Joseph McGuinness increased pressure on the British government to release those still incarcerated, and the following month it was announced that the remaining prisoners were to be released unconditionally.

10   Cumann na mBan was the women's organisation formed in 1914 to work alongside the Irish Volunteers.

11   Corr (2016), pp. 259–66.

12   *Ibid*.

13   Bishop Hoare was personally involved in a divisive campaign which ultimately resulted in the selection of Patrick McKenna

as the IPP candidate for the Longford by-election.

14   UCD Archive, Éamon de Valera papers, P150/1755, correspondence between Fr Ryans and de Valera dated 17 January 1925.

15   Ardagh & Clonmacnois Diocesan Records, anonymous letter dated 21 September 1920 and letter dated 4 October 1920 from Fr Ryans to Bishop Hoare.

16   *Ibid.*, letter dated 20 December 1920, Fr Ryans to Bishop Hoare. Priests were not paid a set amount, surviving instead on a division of the pooled parish income, minus expenses, with the parish priest getting a slightly larger share. Parish income came in the form of Easter and Christmas dues, funeral and christening offerings and other payments for saying Mass in people's homes and administering the sacraments. Kelly, Francis, *Window on a Catholic Parish: St Mary's, Granard, Co. Longford, 1933–68* (Dublin, Irish Academic Press, 1996), p. 18.

17   National Archives of Ireland, DE14/13, letter from Michael Reilly, founder member Aughavas Sinn Féin.

18   UCD Archive, Éamon de Valera papers, P150/1755, correspondence between Fr Ryans and de Valera dated 17 January 1925.

19   Leitrim County Library, T. W. Muldoon, tape 102. On 4 February 1993, Paddy Muldoon's nephew Thomas William Muldoon, then aged seventy-seven, was interviewed by Evelyn Kelly of Leitrim County Library for the Local Studies Department and he provided a detailed account of his lifelong quest for justice in respect of his uncle's death. The Tubman information comes from T. W. Muldoon.

20   Ardagh & Clonmacnois Diocesan Records, letter dated 20 December 1920, Fr Ryans to Bishop Hoare.

21   *Ibid.*, letter dated 31 January 1921, Fr Ryans to Bishop Hoare.

22   *The Leitrim Advertiser*, 26 January 1922.

23   *The Irish Times*, 2 April 1923.

24 The terms of the Treaty included the withdrawal of British forces, which resulted in conflict between pro- and anti-Treaty elements of the IRA to gain control of vacated British barracks and abandoned arms. This situation was further complicated when anti-Treaty forces occupied the capital's Four Courts building in April 1922. Following an ultimatum to the anti-Treaty forces to leave the building, which was refused, the bombardment commenced on 28 June 1922.

25 Muldoon/Donnelly family records: grandchildren.

26 UCD Archive, Seán Mac Eoin papers, P151/214(17), undated prison correspondence March/April 1923, from Fr Ryans to Seán Mac Eoin (the Mac Eoin papers contain a number of letters relating to the Fr Ryans case).

Chapter 3

1 Census Ireland 1911. The arrival of the local narrow gauge railway to the area in the 1880s had allowed for easier transportation of livestock to and from local fairs, and smallholdings in this part of the north midlands began to earn a reasonable living.

2 UCD Archives, Seán Mac Eoin papers, P151/214/17, undated prison correspondence March/April 1923 from Fr Ryans to Seán Mac Eoin.

3 Luddy, Maria, 'Sex and the Single Girl in 1920s and 1930s Ireland', *The Irish Review*, No. 35, 2007, p. 82.

4 *Ibid*, p. 81.

5 Rose Brown Birth Certificate, Dublin Registrars, District No. 4.

6 Executions of anti-Treaty prisoners had led to ever more savage reprisals and further killings from the end of 1922 and into 1923. Thirty-four anti-Treaty prisoners alone were executed during January 1923. In total, at least seventy-seven executions were carried out on anti-Treaty prisoners during the conflict.

7   Ó Súilleabháin, Cormac, *Leitrim's Republican Story 1900–2000* (Leitrim, Cumann Cabhrach Liatroma, 2014), p. 149.

8   *The Anglo Celt*, 3 February 1923.

9   Muldoon/Donnelly family records: Rita Muldoon personal account.

10 Military Archives, Bridget Doherty, Military Service Pensions Collection (henceforth MSPC) MSP34REF43944.

11 Military Archives, John Charles Keegan, MSPC MSP34 REF33962.

12 *Ibid.*, Bridget Doherty, MSPC MSP34REF43944.

13 *Ibid.*

14 Muldoon/Donnelly family records: Rita Muldoon personal account.

15 *Ibid.*

16 *Ibid.*

17 Dáil Debates, 8 February 1923, www.oireachtas.ie/en/debates/debate/dail/1923-02-08/6/#spk_90.

18 *Ibid.*

19 *Ibid.*

Chapter 4

1   *Thom's Official Directory of Great Britain and Ireland for the Year 1923.* An almanac listing street names, businesses, houses etc., Dublin Street section, p. 1569.

2   Ardagh & Clonmacnois Diocesan Record, deposition, City Sessions Court, 16 February, The King v Kate Browne [*sic*] and Rev. Edward Ryan [*sic*].

3   Parnell Square is where the memorial Garden of Remembrance is situated.

4   Ardagh & Clonmacnois Diocesan Records, deposition, City Sessions Court, 16 February, The King v Kate Browne [*sic*] and Rev. Edward Ryan [*sic*].

5   *Ibid.*

6   *The Irish Times*, 10 May 1923.

7   Ardagh & Clonmacnois Diocesan Records, deposition, City Sessions Court, 16 February, The King v Kate Browne [*sic*] and Rev. Edward Ryan [*sic*].

8   *Ibid.*

9   *Ibid.*

10 *Ibid.*

11 UCD Archives, Seán Mac Eoin papers, P151/214(17), undated prison correspondence March/April 1923, Fr Ryans to Seán McEoin [*sic*].

12 Ardagh & Clonmacnois Diocesan Records, deposition, City Sessions Court, 16 February, The King v Kate Browne and Rev. Edward Ryan [*sic*].

Chapter 5

1   Muldoon/Donnelly family records: Rita Muldoon personal account.

2   *Ibid.*

3   *Ibid.*

4   *Ibid.*

5   *Ibid.*

6   *Ibid.*

7   *Ibid.* The 20 February entry in Rita's personal account reads: 'Bishop in Aughavas, Suspended Fr. R.'; and later immediately prior to 18 March murder entry: 'He removed some belongings from curate's residence to a private house (Mrs. Flyns [*sic*]) in Aughavas but never removed all his things nor handed key to p.p.'

8   *Ibid.*

9   *Ibid.*

10 *Ibid.*

11 UCD Archives, Seán Mac Eoin papers, P151/3/23.

12 Dáil Debates, 8 February 1923, www.oireachtas.ie/en/debates/debate/dail/1923-02-08/6/#spk_90.

Chapter 6

1   Interview with Thomas Melia, local historian, 2 December 2017.
2   Ardagh & Clonmacnois Diocesan Records, Biographical. Fr Masterson had been president of St Mel's College, a position held many years earlier by Bishop Hoare.
3   *Leitrim Observer*, 24 March 1923. Inquest Report.
4   Mahon, Frank, 'A Resilient People', *Leitrim Guardian*, 1995, p. 96. It would be another four years before the establishment of the Electricity Supply Board (ESB) and the creation of a proper public electricity network in Ireland.
5   *Leitrim Observer*, 24 March 1923. Inquest Report.
6   *Ibid.*
7   *Ibid.*
8   Kerr/Courtney family account.
9   Muldoon/Donnelly family records: Rita Muldoon personal account.
10 Muldoon/Donnelly family records: grandchildren.
11 Muldoon/Donnelly family records: Rita Muldoon personal account.
12 *Ibid.*
13 Military Archives, National Army Report A/122, Mohill, 18 March 1923.

Chapter 7

1   *Leitrim Observer*, 24 March 1923. Inquest Report.
2   *Ibid.*
3   Interview with Thomas Melia, local historian, 2 December 2017.
4   *Longford Leader*, 7 June 1924.
5   *Leitrim Observer*, 24 March 1923. Inquest Report.
6   Muldoon/Donnelly family records: Rita Muldoon personal account.
7   *The Leitrim Advertiser*, 5 April 1923.

8   *Irish Independent*, 29 March 1923.
9   Muldoon/Donnelly family records: Rita Muldoon personal account.
10 Leitrim County Library, T. W. Muldoon, tape 102.
11 Muldoon/Donnelly family records: Rita Muldoon personal account.
12 *The Leitrim Advertiser*, 5 April 1923.
13 Muldoon/Donnelly family records: letter dated 'Easter Monday' (2 April 1923), Tom Reynolds to Amby (Ambrose Lee).
14 See Ó Súilleabháin (2014), p. 154, for additional evidence that Fr Ryans was attempting to have Mary Kate Gallogly committed to a mental hospital.
15 *Irish Independent*, 19 April 1923.
16 Royal College of Physicians of Ireland Archives: Muldoon, Michael Patrick.
17 *The Leitrim Advertiser*, 5 April 1923.
18 Kerr/Courtney family account.

Chapter 8

1   Leitrim County Library, Dr Muldoon, file no. 502, murder investigation. Copies of the correspondence relating to the initial investigation into Paddy Muldoon's murder are to be found in this file in Leitrim County Library, Ballinamore. They were possibly provided to the library by Thomas William Muldoon in connection with his taped interview of 4 February 1993, ref. tape no. 102.
2   Leitrim County Library, Dr Muldoon, file no. 502, murder investigation, letter dated 20 March 1923, Inspector Wm. Breen to The Supt., Sligo.
3   Muldoon/Donnelly family records: Rita Muldoon personal papers, copy of death certificate dated 28 May 1923, Thos. Redahan, medical officer.

4   Leitrim County Library, Dr Muldoon, file no. 502, murder investigation, letter dated 23 March 1923 from Inspector Wm. Breen (signing for The Supt., Sligo) to the Commissioner, Civic Guard, Phoenix Park.

5   Muldoon/Donnelly family records: Rita Muldoon personal papers, letter dated 18 April 1923, Ambrose Lee to George Lynch.

6   Leitrim County Library, Dr Muldoon, file no. 502, murder investigation, Éamon O'Cugain, Leas Commissioner, to the Supt. Sligo.

7   *Ibid.*, report dated 3 April 1923 and signed by R. Muldoon, Supt. This document is likely to be a transcript of the requested Form 38.

8   The document in total covers a ten-week period from mid-January to the end of March 1923. By its nature we can take it that she viewed the final entry as very significant, comparable in importance to the first entry describing Fr Ryans' production of an automatic pistol.

9   Muldoon/Donnelly family records: Rita Muldoon personal account.

10 *The Irish Times*, 2 April 1923.

11 The attack on Ballyconnell was a revenge action triggered by the shooting dead of Michael Cull, one of the leaders of the Arigna column, in an earlier armed raid in the town. The attack left two unarmed civilians dead and the townsfolk traumatised. One resident reported a shop owner being wounded in the leg and his assistant being shot dead for resisting the attackers. A teacher from Galway staying in the town was also shot down in cold blood. Women and children were frantically seeking shelter from bullets and bomb shrapnel as the attackers continued their fifteen-minute onslaught (*Leitrim Observer*, 10 February 1923). Within a week the National Army responded with a major offensive.

12 *The Irish Times*, 2 April 1923. No explanation is given in the newspaper report as to why the two men were not detained. The fact that they voluntarily surrendered may have been a factor. If a man surrendered, as opposed to being captured in arms, handed over his weapons and signed a declaration to the effect that he would not take up arms again, in most cases he was allowed to go free, presumably if there were no other charges outstanding against him.

13 *The Irish Times*, 2 April 1923.

14 UCD Archives, Seán Mac Eoin papers, P151/214(20), letter dated 18 April 1923, Command Legal Staff Officer to Maj. General McKeon [*sic*], GOC.

15 Leitrim County Library, Dr Muldoon, file no. 502, murder investigation, letter dated 16 April 1923, R. Ua Maolchatha, Aire Chosanta (R. Mulcahy, minister for defence) to the minister for home affairs (contains Mac Eoin report).

16 *Ibid.*, letter dated 16 April 1923, R. Ua Maolchatha, Aire Chosanta (R. Mulcahy, minister for defence), to the minister for home affairs.

17 Muldoon/Donnelly family records: grandchildren; Ó Súilleabháin (2014), p. 149.

18 In June 1922 Michael Collins attended Mac Eoin's wedding to Alice Cooney at St Mel's cathedral in Longford, an event of such significance that it featured in film coverage by Pathé News.

19 Leitrim County Library, Dr Muldoon, file no. 502, murder investigation, letter dated 22 May 1923, P. M. Moynihan, Director, C.I.D., to The Secretary, Ministry of Home Affairs.

20 *Ibid.*

21 Ardagh & Clonmacnois Diocesan Records, letter dated 10 June 1921, Fr Ryans to Bishop Hoare with Bishop Hoare's response annotated thereon.

22 Ardagh & Clonmacnois Diocesan Records, biographical.

23 Leitrim County Library, Dr Muldoon, file no. 502, murder investigation, letter dated 22 May 1923, P. M. Moynihan, Director, C.I.D., to The Secretary, Ministry of Home Affairs.

24 Military Archives, John Charles Keegan, MSPC MSP34 REF33962.

25 Leitrim County Library, Dr Muldoon, file no. 502, murder investigation, letter dated 22 May 1923, P. M. Moynihan, Director, C.I.D., to The Secretary, Ministry of Home Affairs.

26 Muldoon/Donnelly family records: Rita Muldoon personal papers, letter dated 5 April 1923, P. Hogan, Ministry of Agriculture, to Ambrose Lee. The head of government of the new state was given the title of president; it wasn't until 1937 that the current title of Taoiseach was introduced.

27 White, Terence de Vere, *Kevin O'Higgins* (Cork, Anvil Books, 1987), pp. 133 and 153.

28 Muldoon/Donnelly family records: Rita Muldoon personal papers, letter dated 9 April 1923, P. Hogan, Ministry of Agriculture to Ambrose Lee.

29 *Ibid.*, letter dated 11 April 1923, Ambrose Lee to Patrick Hogan, minister for agriculture (addressed 'My dear Hogan').

Chapter 9

1 Ardagh & Clonmacnois Diocesan Records, letter dated 20 December 1920, Fr Ryans to Bishop Hoare.

2 *Leitrim Observer*, 24 April 1920.

3 Ó Súilleabháin (2014), p. 55.

4 Leitrim County Library, Francis Curran, Augharan, file no. 1303.

5 *Leitrim Observer*, 24 April 1920.

6 Ardagh & Clonmacnois Diocesan Records, letter dated 20 December 1920, Fr Ryans to Bishop Hoare. See also Leeson, David M., *The Black & Tans* (Oxford, Oxford University Press, 2011), pp. 158–164.

7 *Ibid.*, anonymous letter dated 21 September 1920 to My Lord Bishop (Hoare).

8 *Leitrim Observer*, 16 October 1920.

9 Ardagh & Clonmacnois Diocesan Records, letter dated 20 December 1920, Fr Ryans to Bishop Hoare.

10 *Ibid.*, letter dated 11 February 1921, Fr Ryans to Bishop Hoare.

11 *Ibid.*

12 *Ibid.*, letter dated 10 June 1921, Fr Ryans to Bishop Hoare.

13 Ardagh & Clonmacnois Diocesan Records, Biographical/ Mrs Flynn had a brother, Fr Donohoe, a priest and also a half brother, Fr Reynolds, a priest. Mrs Flynn was also related to Bishop Hoare.

Chapter 10

1 UCD Archives, Seán Mac Eoin papers, P151/214 (3), letter dated 6 July 1925, Seán Mac Eoin to Chief of Staff, General Headquarters.

2 UCD Archives, Seán Mac Eoin papers, P151/214 (20), letter dated 18 April 1923, Command Legal Staff Officer to Maj. General McKeon [*sic*], GOC.

3 UCD Archives, Seán Mac Eoin papers, P151/214 (3), letter dated 6 July 1925, Seán Mac Eoin to Chief of Staff, General Headquarters, in which Mac Eoin advised him: 'I have a private file which contains some statements of Fr Ryans, which I promised him would not become public property.'

4 UCD Archives, Seán Mac Eoin papers, P151/214 (18), undated prison correspondence March/April 1923, from Fr Ryans to Seán Mac Eoin.

5 UCD Archives, Seán Mac Eoin papers, P151/214 (17), undated prison correspondence March/April 1923, from Fr Ryans to Seán Mac Eoin.

6 Ardagh & Clonmacnois Diocesan Records, deposition, City Sessions Court, 16 February 1923, The King v Kate Browne,

Rev. Edward Ryan [*sic*].

7   UCD Archives, Seán Mac Eoin papers, P151/214 (18), undated prison correspondence March/April 1923, from Fr Ryans to Seán Mac Eoin.

8   *Ibid.*

9   UCD Archives, Seán Mac Eoin papers, P151/214 (13), undated prison correspondence March/April 1923, from Fr Ryans to Seán Mac Eoin.

10 UCD Archives, Seán Mac Eoin papers, P151/214 (14), letter dated 20 April, 1923 Seán Mac Eoin to Rev. Edward Ryan [*sic*].

11 UCD Archives, Seán Mac Eoin papers, P151/214 (3), letter dated 6 July, 1925, Seán Mac Eoin to Chief of Staff, General Headquarters.

Chapter 11

1   Leitrim County Library, Dr Muldoon, file 502, murder investigation, Military Archives, 23rd Battalion Longford, Form B.1., Operation Report, 11 May 1923.

2   Leitrim County Library, Dr Muldoon, file 502, murder investigation, letter dated 22 May 1923, P. M. Moynihan, Director, C.I.D., to The Secretary, Ministry of Home Affairs.

3   *The Irish Times*, 10 May 1923.

4   UCD Archives, Seán Mac Eoin papers, P151/214 (17), undated prison correspondence March/April 1923, Fr Ryans to Seán Mac Eoin.

5   *The Irish Times*, 10 May 1923.

6   *Ibid.*

7   *Ibid.*

8   *Ibid.*

9   *Ibid.*

10 The Ladies Detention Camp was located at Athlone Castle, a few minutes' walk from Major General Mac Eoin's Custume

Barracks headquarters. It was used during the Civil War for the detention of female republican prisoners.

11 Bohan/Brady family records.

12 *Ibid.*

13 *Ibid.*

14 Death Record, Castleknock District, Co. Dublin, Reg. no. 3318949.

15 *The Freeman's Journal*, 15 May 1923.

16 UCD Archives, Seán Mac Eoin papers, P151/214 (16), letter dated 16 May 1923, Fr Ryans to Seán Mac Eoin.

17 UCD Archives, Seán Mac Eoin papers, P151/214 (15), letter dated 21 May 1923, Major Gen. Seán Mac Eoin to Fr T. Meehan.

18 Ardagh & Clonmacnois Diocesan Records, letter dated 26 May 1923, Fr Ryans to Bishop Hoare.

19 *Ibid.*

Chapter 12

1 Death Record, Rowan/Mohill/Leitrim, Reg. no. 3336888.

2 *The Leitrim Advertiser*, 5 April 1923. Maggie Ellis was the proprietor of a general grocers store in Mohill. She was unmarried and by all accounts a very religious woman.

3 Muldoon/Donnelly family records: Rita Muldoon personal papers, letter from Margaret (Maggie) Ellis to Ambrose (Amby) Lee.

4 *The Leitrim Advertiser*, 26 January 1922. In January 1922 Maggie Ellis was re-elected as secretary of the association and Rita Muldoon was re-elected as a committee member.

5 Interview with Thomas Melia, local historian, 2 December 2017.

6 *Ibid.*

7 National Archive, Administration papers, Michael Patrick Muldoon, 19 April 1923, Ref: CS/HC/PO/4/76/5385.

8   Muldoon/Donnelly family records: Rita Muldoon personal papers, letter dated 18 April 1923, Ambrose Lee to George Lynch.

9   *Ibid.*, letter dated 31 July 1923, Hannan & O'Brien, Solicitors, to Mrs Muldoon.

10   RTÉ *Documentary on One*, 'An Unholy Trinity', interview with Michael Muldoon (grandson).

11   *Connacht Tribune*, 12 November 1932.

Chapter 13

1   *Weekly Irish Times*, 21 July 1923.

2   Ardagh & Clonmacnois Diocesan Records, letter dated 18 July 1923, Fr M. S. McMahon to Bishop Hoare.

3   *Irish Independent*, 15 May 1917, and *The Cork Examiner*, 23 November 1926.

4   In the aftermath of the ceasefire the attitude of the government to outstanding Civil War crimes was yet to be seen. The country's finances and economy had been devastated by the cost and destruction of the war and there were huge compensation claims to be met. It was unlikely that the State would have had the resources or indeed the appetite to pursue all outstanding cases.

5   Ardagh & Clonmacnois Diocesan Records, letter dated 18 July 1923, Fr M. S. McMahon to Bishop Hoare.

6   *Leitrim Observer*, 8 March 1919.

7   UCD Archives, Seán Mac Eoin papers, P151/227(9), letter dated 23 July 1923, Capt. Seamus F. Baxter & Capt. Geo. Geraghty to The Most Rev. Dr. Hoare.

8   'Army declared war on sexually transmitted diseases in 1920s', *The Irish Times*, 10 February 2017, www.irishtimes.com/culture/heritage/army-declared-war-on-sexually-transmitted-diseases-in-1920s-1.2969761.

9   UCD Archives, Seán Mac Eoin papers, P151/227(9), letter

dated 23 July 1923, Capt. Seamus F. Baxter & Capt. Geo. Geraghty to The Most Rev. Dr. Hoare.

10 UCD Archives, Seán Mac Eoin papers, P151/227(3), letter dated 28 July 1923, Seán Mac Eoin, GOC Athlone Command, to Most Rev Dr Hoare, Lord Bishop of Ardagh & Clonmacnois.

11 *Ibid.*

12 UCD Archives, Seán Mac Eoin papers, P151/227(2), letter dated 30 July 1923, Bishop Hoare to 'My dear General'.

13 *Ibid.*

14 *Weekly Irish Times*, 18 August 1923.

15 Death Record, Castleknock District, Co. Dublin, Reg. no. 3318949.

16 *The Freeman's Journal* and *Irish Independent*, 9 May 1923.

17 *Ibid.*, 10 May 1923.

18 *Leitrim Observer*, 12 May 1923; *The Freeman's Journal*, 15 May 1923.

Chapter 14

1   USA Naturalisation Declaration, 17 January 1927.

2   Leitrim County Library, Charlie Eddie McGoohan memoirs.

3   Muldoon/Donnelly family records, undated and unsigned handwritten draft response to IRA Publicity Dept. statement dated 15 May 1924.

4   Leitrim County Library, T. W. Muldoon, tape 102.

5   UCD Archives, Seán Mac Eoin papers, P151/201(14 & 15), two-page General Monthly Report dated 26 May 1923, from Headquarters, 23rd Infantry Battalion, Longford to G.O.C. Athlone Command.

6   Military Archives, Edward Fitzgerald, MSPC 3D20.

7   *Leitrim Observer*, 24 March 1923.

8   Military Archives, John Charles Keegan, Medals Ref. MD41616.

9   Fitzgerald family source.

10 *Leitrim Observer*, 31 March 1923.

11 Military Archives, National Army, 23rd Battalion Longford, Operation Report, 31 March 1923.

12 *Leitrim Observer*, 31 March 1923.

13 O'Malley, Ernie, *Rising Out: Seán Connolly of Longford*, 1890–1921 (Dublin, UCD Press, 2015), Appendix 1, pp. 171–72.

14 Leitrim County Library, J. C. Keegan, file no. 1869.

15 Military Archives, John Charles Keegan, Medals Ref. MD41616.

16 *Leitrim Observer*, 31 March 1923.

17 *The Freeman's Journal*, 2 and 3 May 1923.

18 Military Archives, Mary Kate McDermott, MSPC MSP34 REF41708.

19 *Leitrim Observer*, 19 May 1923.

20 *Ibid.*

21 *Leitrim Observer*, 26 May 1923.

22 National Army General Weekly Return (Irregular) 24 May, 22nd/23rd Battalions, Boyle & Longford.

23 Military Archives, Patrick Keville, MSPC DP24313.

24 UCD Archives, Seán Mac Eoin papers, P151/201 (14 & 15), two-page General Monthly Report dated 26 May 1923, from Headquarters, 23rd Infantry Battalion, Longford to GOC Athlone Command.

25 No National Army documents have been unearthed that connect Keegan to the Fitzgerald killing. However, his family were of the opinion that Keegan was involved. Their basis for that belief was that, in the locality, it was well known who was out and armed on any given night.

26 National Army General Weekly Return, 22nd/23rd Battalions, 17 August 1923.

27 *Ibid.*, 24 August 1923.

28 *Ibid.*, 21 September 1923.

29 *Ibid.*, 26 October 1923.

30 Military Archives, John Charles Keegan, Medals Ref. MD41616.

31 *Leitrim Observer*, 1 March 1924.

32 *Ibid.*

33 Military Archives, MSPC, Patrick Joseph Kane, 4D58.

34 *Ibid.*

35 *Ibid.*

36 Military Archives, John Charles Keegan, Medals Ref. MD41616.

37 Military Archives, Patrick Joseph Kane, MSPC 4D58.

38 *Ibid.*

39 *Ibid.*

40 *Ibid.*

41 *Ibid.*

42 *Ibid.*

43 Keegan later claimed he was armed and that Kane was shot by his own men while attempting to escape to safety. Keegan hid his revolver and IRA papers in a chimney prior to surrendering. Military Archives, John Charles Keegan, Medals Ref. MD41616.

44 Military Archives, Patrick Joseph Kane, MSPC 4D58.

45 *Ibid.*

46 For example, *The Irish Times*, 26 March 1924; *Longford Leader*, 29 March 1924; *The Freeman's Journal*, 27 March 1924; *The Cork Examiner*, 26 March 1924.

47 Military Archives, Patrick Joseph Kane, MSPC 4D58.

48 Military Archives, John Charles Keegan, MSPC MSP34 REF33962.

49 National Army, General Monthly Report, 26 May 1923, 23rd Infantry Battalion, Longford.

50 *Irish Independent*, 13 November 1924.

Chapter 15

1 UCD Archives, Éamon de Valera papers, P150/1755, letter dated 17 January 1925, Fr Ryans to Éamon de Valera.

2 *Ibid.*

3 *Ibid.* Thomas William Muldoon is the only source who names all three, John Charlie Keegan, Cassels from outside Mohill and Clyne from Ballinamore. In *Leitrim's Fighting Story*, Cormac Ó Súilleabháin names John Charlie Keegan and Willie Cassells of Gorvagh as two of the three men involved in the attack.

4 David Plunkett Papers (this collection includes items from the Maurice 'Moss' Twomey archive), letter dated 30 April 1924, P. O'B O/C (Frank O'Beirne) to C/S (Chief of Staff).

5 *Ibid.*

6 *Longford Leader*, 17 May 1924, and David Plunkett Papers, statement dated 15 May 1925, issued by Publicity Dept., Irish Republican Army.

7 *Irish Independent*, 19 May 1924.

8 *Longford Leader*, 7 June 1924.

9 *Ibid.* Rita references the entry wound at the collar bone. Other accounts refer to the exit wound at the neck area.

10 Muldoon/Donnelly Records, copy of death certificate for Dr M. P. Muldoon issued 28 May 1923 by Thos. Redahan, Medical Officer, present at death. Also from Leitrim County Library, Dr Muldoon, file no. 502.

11 *Longford Leader*, 7 June 1924.

12 Muldoon/Donnelly Records, draft undated letter to The Editor, *Irish Independent*, in response to IRA publicity department statement in *Irish Independent* 17th inst. (17 May 1924).

13 *The Irish Times*, 2 April 1923.

14 David Plunkett Papers, letter dated 18 June 1924, Fr Ryans to Chief of Staff IRA.

15 UCD Archives, Éamon de Valera papers, P150/1755, letter dated 17 January 1925, Fr Ryans to Éamon de Valera.

16 After his release from Arbour Hill Prison Éamon de Valera returned to his position as president of Sinn Féin, the political wing of the republican movement which had been defeated in the recent Civil War. It was not until March 1926 that he, and others, would split from Sinn Féin, on account of its continuing abstentionist policy, to found a new republican party, Fianna Fáil. The new party, notwithstanding the contentious oath of allegiance, would eventually commit to entering Dáil Éireann.

17 UCD Archives, Éamon de Valera papers, P150/1755, letter dated 17 January 1925, Fr Ryans to Éamon de Valera.

18 *Ibid.*

19 *Ibid.*

20 O'Malley, Ernie, *The Men Will Talk To Me: Mayo Interviews* (Cork, Mercier Press, 2014), pp. 326.

21 *Ibid.*, pp. 324–5. Keegan is mistakenly referred to as 'Dignan' in the text; this may be a result of O'Malley's notoriously bad handwriting, or because Tom Carney's memory was a little faulty. Despite this, there can be no doubt that he's referring to Keegan.

22 *Ibid.*, p. 326.

23 Mac Eoin's report copied by Mulcahy to the minister for home affairs, 16 April 1923, states, referring to the three men who committed the murder and whose leader was Keegan, 'Father Ryans met these fellows in Cattan, picked them up and took them back to Mohill'.

24 O'Malley (2014), pp. 326–27.

25 UCD Archives, Éamon de Valera papers, P150/1755, letter dated 17 January 1925, Fr Ryans to Éamon de Valera.

26 *Ibid.*

27 *Ibid.*

28 *Ibid.*, letter dated 17 January 1925 [*sic*] on behalf of the President (Sinn Féin) to B. O'Brennan [*sic*] with annotation signed 'R. O'B'.

29 UCD Archives, Éamon de Valera papers, P150/1755, letter dated 22 January 1925, Chief of Staff, IRA to Éamon de Valera.

Chapter 16

1   UCD Archives, Éamon de Valera papers, P150/1755, report dated 26 July 1924, from 'K' (Seán Lemass) to C/S (Frank Aiken, IRA Chief of Staff).

2   Garvin, Tom, *Judging Lemass* (Dublin, Royal Irish Academy, 2009), pp. 106–7. Also David Plunkett Papers, various.

3   Garvin (2009), p. 265.

4   UCD Archives, Éamon de Valera papers, P150/1755, letter dated 27 January 1925, Secretary to the President, Sinn Féin, to Rev. E. Ryans.

5   *Leitrim Observer*, 28 February 1925.

6   Carroll, Denis, *They Have Fooled You Again: Michael O'Flanagan, 1876–1942* (Dublin, Columba Press, 1993), p. 149.

7   *Leitrim Observer*, 28 February 1925.

8   *Irish Independent*, 27 February 1925.

9   *Ibid.*, 2 March 1925.

10 Muldoon/Donnelly records, letter dated 7 March 1925, Asst. Secretary, Dept. of Justice to R. Ambrose Lee.

11 Leitrim County Library, J. C. Keegan, file no. 1869. The library purchased this single letter of Keegan's from the same auction of Maurice 'Moss' Twomey archive material which provided the David Plunkett Papers (see endnote 4, Chapter 15). It is likely therefore that the Keegan letter was originally part of the IRA Muldoon investigation file acquired by David Plunkett.

12 Military Archives, John Charles Keegan, Medals Ref. MD41616.

13 UCD Archives, Éamon de Valera papers, P150/1755.

14 Mac Eoin, Uinseann, *The IRA in the Twilight Years, 1923–1948* (Dublin, Argenta Press, 1997), p. 115.

15 *Irish Independent*, 11 July 1925.

16 *The Irish Times*, 2 April 1923.

17 Military Archives, Margaret McKeon, MSPC MSP34 REF62098.

18 UCD Archives, Seán Mac Eoin papers, P151/214, letter dated 17 June 1925, Canon P. Donohoe to Major Gen. Seán McKeon [*sic*].

19 UCD Archives, Seán Mac Eoin papers, P151/214 (7), letter dated 19 June 1925, Major General Seán Mac Eoin to The Very Revd. Canon P. Donohoe.

20 UCD Archives, Mac Eoin papers, P151/214 (3), letter dated 6 July 1925, Major General Seán Mac Eoin to Chief of Staff, General Headquarters.

21 UCD Archives, Seán Mac Eoin papers, P151/214 (3) & P151/214 (8), letter dated 19 June 1925, Major General Seán Mac Eoin to Chief of Staff, General Headquarters.

22 National Archives, Office of the Attorney General, compensation claim, Rev. E. Ryans, AGO/1/72.

23 *Ibid.*

24 UCD Archives, Seán Mac Eoin papers, P151/214(1).

25 www.libertyellisfoundation.org/passenger search/Edward Ryans.

26 www.libertyellisfoundation.org/passenger search/John C. Keegan.

27 *The Cork Examiner*, 29 October 1925.

28 *Leitrim Observer*, 14 November 1925.

Chapter 17

1 Muldoon/Donnelly family records.

2 *Ibid.*, letter dated 14 May 1925, addressed 'Dear Sir' from C. Cloherty, Clerk of the Peace, Courthouse, Galway.

3 *Kerry News*, 15 October 1926; *Longford Leader*, 16 October 1926.

4 Leitrim County Library, T. W. Muldoon, tape no. 102.

5 *Ibid.*

6 *Ibid.*; *Leitrim Observer*, 24 March 1923.

7   Leitrim County Library, Dr Muldoon, file no. 502, murder investigation, letter dated 16 April 1923, Richard Mulcahy, minister of defence to the minister for home affairs.

8   Leitrim County Library, T. W. Muldoon, tape no. 102.

9   *Irish Independent*, 13 November 1924.

10 Leitrim County Library, T. W. Muldoon, tape no. 102.

11 *Ibid*.

12 Muldoon/Donnelly family records.

13 Muldoon/Faulkner family records, letter dated 9 August 1995, Desmond Muldoon to Thomas William Muldoon.

14 Muldoon/Donnelly family records.

15 Leitrim County Library, T. W. Muldoon, tape no. 102.

16 *Ibid*.

17 *Ibid*.

18 The title of the ministry for home affairs was changed to the ministry for justice in June 1924.

19 Leitrim County Library, T. W. Muldoon, tape no. 102.

20 *Ibid*.

21 *Orlando Evening Star*, 17 June 1928.

22 Palmer family (Mohill) records.

23 Ardagh & Clonmacnois Diocesan Records, letter dated 15 April 1936, Canon Masterson to The Most Rev. Dr McNamee.

24 Leitrim County Library, T. W. Muldoon, tape no. 102.

25 *Longford Leader*, 24 June 1922.

26 UCD Archives, Seán Mac Eoin papers, P1151/218(5).

Chapter 18

1   Military Archives, John Charles Keegan, MSPC MSP34 REF33962.

2   *Ibid*.

3   *Ibid*.

4   Muldoon/Donnelly family records.

5   Leitrim County Library, T. W. Muldoon, tape no. 102.

6   *Ibid.*

7   *Ibid.* and interview with Joe Griffin, Muldoon relative.

8   *Ibid.*

9   *Ibid.*

10 *Ibid.*

11 *Ibid.*

12 Leitrim County Library, Dr Muldoon, file no. 502.

13 Leitrim County Library, T. W. Muldoon, tape no. 102.

14 *Ibid.*

15 *Ibid.*

16 *Ibid.*

17 General Register Office England/Registration District Lancaster, County of Lancaster.

18 Military Archives, John Charles Keegan, Medals Ref. MD41616.

19 Leitrim County Library, T. W. Muldoon, tape no. 102.

20 *Ibid.*

21 Leitrim County Library, Dr Muldoon, file no. 502.

22 Interview with Padraig Leyden, local historian.

23 Leitrim County Library, T. W. Muldoon, tape no. 102.

Chapter 19

1   UCD Archives, Éamon de Valera papers, P150/1755, letter dated 17 January 1925, Fr Ryans to Éamon de Valera.

2   Ardagh & Clonmacnois Diocesan Records, biographical.

3   Muldoon/Donnelly family records.

4   Ardagh & Clonmacnois Diocesan Records, anonymous letter dated 21 September 1920 to 'My Lord Bishop' (Hoare).

5   Ardagh & Clonmacnois Diocesan Records, letters.

6   *Ibid.*

7   Leitrim County Library, T. W. Muldoon, tape no. 102.

8   Leitrim County Library, Dr Muldoon, file no. 502, murder investigation, letter dated 16 April 1923, R. Ua Maolchatha,

Aire Chosanta (R. Mulcahy, minister for defence) to the minister for home affairs (contains the Mac Eoin report).

9 Muldoon/Donnelly family records: Rita Muldoon personal account.

10 UCD Archives, Seán Mac Eoin papers, P151/214 (3), letter dated 6 July 1925, Major General Mac Eoin to Chief of Staff, General Headquarters.

11 Muldoon/Donnelly family records.

12 UCD Archives, Éamon de Valera papers, P150/1755; David Plunkett papers.

13 *Irish Independent*, 3 March 1925.

14 UCD Archives, Éamon de Valera papers, P150/1755.

15 Dorney, John, *The Civil War in Dublin: The Fight for the Irish Capital 1922–1924* (Dublin, Merrion Press, 2017), p. 260.

16 Leitrim County Library, J. C. Keegan, file no. 1869.

17 Military Archives, John Charles Keegan, Medals Ref. MD41616.

18 UCD Archives, Éamon de Valera papers, P150/1755.

Epilogue

1 Mac Eoin (1997), pp. 70–124.

2 UCD Archives, Seán Mac Eoin papers; Military Archives, MSPC, various.

3 *The Irish Press*, 18 March 1936.

4 Muldoon/Donnelly family records: grandchildren; interview with Michael Muldoon (grandson) in the RTÉ *Documentary on One*, 'An Unholy Trinity'.

5 *Ibid.*

6 *Ibid.*

7 Clongowes College Archives, Clane, Co. Kildare: Desmond & Patrick Muldoon fees.

8 Muldoon/Faulkner family records, letter dated 3 February 1997, Des Muldoon to Thomas William Muldoon.

9   Muldoon/Faulkner family records, letter dated 9 August 1995, Des Muldoon to Thomas William Muldoon.

10 Muldoon/Donnelly family records: Rita Muldoon personal account.

11 Military Archives, Margaret McKeon, MSPC MSP34 REF62098.

12 *Ibid.*

13 *Ibid.*

14 Military Archives, John Charles Keegan, Medals Ref. MD41616.

15 Interview with David Logan following his conversation with the Moran brothers, 15 August 2017.

16 Ó Súilleabháin (2014), p. 161.

17 White (1987), p. 256.

18 Military Archives, John Charles Keegan, Medals Ref. MD41616.

19 Birth Register, Mohill, Co. Leitrim, 05248621/171.

20 Ó Súilleabháin (2014), p. 161.

21 McCarthy, John P., *Kevin O'Higgins: Builder of the Irish State* (Dublin, Irish Academic Press, 2006), p. 17.

22 Muldoon/Donnelly family records.

23 Muldoon/Donnelly family records. The song was first recorded by John McCormack in 1919.

BIBLIOGRAPHY

Published Sources

Breen, Dan, *My Fight for Irish Freedom* (Dublin, Anvil, 1981)

Carroll, Denis, *They Have Fooled You Again: Michael O'Flanagan, 1876–1942* (Dublin, Columbia Press, 1993)

Casey, Patrick J., Cullen, Kevin T. and Duignan, Joe P., *Irish Doctors in the First World War* (Sallins, Merrion Press, 2015)

Clarke, Gemma, *Everyday Violence in the Irish Civil War* (Cambridge, Cambridge University Press, 2014)

Coleman, Marie, *County Longford and the Irish Revolution, 1910–1923* (Dublin, Irish Academic Press, 2003)

Coogan, Tim Pat, *Michael Collins: A Biography* (London, Hutchinson, 1990)

Coogan, Tim Pat, *The Twelve Apostles: Michael Collins, the Squad and Ireland's Fight for Freedom* (London, Head of Zeus, 2016)

Corr, Elizabeth, 'Up Longford', *Teathbha: Journal of County Longford Historical Society*, Vol. IV, No. 3, 2016, pp. 259–66

Dooley, Chris, *Redmond: A Life Undone* (Dublin, Gill & Macmillan, 2015)

Dorney, John, *The Civil War in Dublin: The Fight for the Irish Capital 1922–1924* (Newbridge, Merrion Press, 2017)

Durney, James, *The Civil War in Kildare* (Cork, Mercier Press, 2011)

Fanning, Ronan, *Éamon de Valera: A Will To Power* (London, Faber & Faber, 2016)

Ferriter, Diarmuid, *A Nation and Not A Rabble: The Irish Revolution 1913–1923* (London, Profile Books, 2015)

Foley, Michael, *The Bloodied Field: The Croke Park Killings on Bloody*

Sunday (Dublin, The O'Brien Press, 2015)

Garvin, Tom, *Nationalist Revolutionaries in Ireland 1858–1928* (Oxford, Clarendon Press, 1987)

Garvin, Tom, *Judging Lemass* (Dublin, Royal Irish Academy, 2009)

Harrington, Niall C., *Kerry Landing: August 1922* (Dublin, Anvil, 1992)

Heffernan, Brian, *Freedom and the Fifth Commandment: Catholic Priests and Political Violence in Ireland, 1919–21* (Manchester, Manchester University Press, 2016)

Keane, Fergal, *Wounds: A Memoir of Love and War* (London, William Collins, 2017)

Kelly, Francis, *Window on a Catholic Parish: St Mary's, Granard, Co. Longford, 1933–68* (Dublin, Irish Academic Press, 1996)

Killeen, Richard, *A Short History of the Irish Revolution 1912 to 1927* (Dublin, Gill & Macmillan, 2007)

Laffan, Michael, *Judging W.T. Cosgrave* (Dublin, Royal Irish Academy, 2014)

Leeson, David M., *The Black & Tans: British Police and Auxiliaries in the Irish War of Independence* (Oxford, Oxford University Press, 2011)

Leyden, Padraig, *Fenagh: The GAA Story* (Fenagh, Fenagh GAA Club, 1985)

Luddy, Maria, 'Sex and the Single Girl in 1920s and 1930s Ireland', *The Irish Review*, No. 35, 2007, pp. 79–91

Mac Eoin, Uinseann, *Survivors: the story of Ireland's struggle as told through some of her outstanding living people recalling events from the days of Davitt, through James Connolly, Brugha, Collins, Liam Mellows, and Rory O'Connor, to the present time* (Dublin, Argenta, 1980)

Mac Eoin, Uinseann, *The IRA in the Twilight Years: 1923–1948* (Dublin, Argenta, 1997)

McCarthy, John P., *Kevin O'Higgins: Builder of the Irish State* (Dublin, Irish Academic Press, 2006)

Murray, Patrick, *Oracles of God: The Roman Catholic Church and Irish Politics, 1922–1937* (Dublin, UCD Press, 2000)

Neeson, Eoin, *The Civil War 1922–23* (Dublin, Poolbeg, 1995)

O'Connor, Frank, *The Big Fellow: Michael Collins and the Irish Revolution* (Cork, Mercier, 2018)

O'Malley, Ernie, *The Men Will Talk to Me: Mayo Interviews*, ed. Cormac K.H. O'Malley and Vincent Keane (Cork, Mercier Press, 2014)

O'Malley, Ernie, *Rising Out: Seán Connolly of Longford, 1890–1921* (Dublin, UCD Press, 2015)

Ó Ruairc, Pádraig Óg, *Revolution: A Photographic History of Revolutionary Ireland, 1913–1923* (Cork, Mercier Press, 2011)

Ó Ruairc, Pádraig Óg, *Truce: Murder, Myth and the Last Days of the Irish War of Independence* (Cork, Mercier Press, 2016)

Ó Súilleabháin, Cormac, *Leitrim's Republican Story, 1900–2000* (Leitrim, Cumann Cabhrach Liatroma, 2014)

Price, Dominic, *We Bled Together: Michael Collins, The Squad and the Dublin Brigade* (Cork, Collins Press, 2017)

Slevin, Fiona, *By Hereditary Virtues: A History of Lough Rynn* (Coolabawn Publishing, 2006)

Thom's Official Directory of Great Britain and Ireland for the Year 1923 (Dublin, Alex Thom and Co., 1923)

Tobin, Fergal, *The Irish Revolution: An Illustrated History, 1912–1925* (Dublin, Gill & Macmillan, 2013)

Whelan, Michael, *The Parish of Aughavas: Its History and its People* (Co. Offaly, Brosna Press, 1998)

White, Terence de Vere, *Kevin O'Higgins* (Dublin, Anvil Books, 1987)

Unpublished Sources

McGarty, Patrick, 'Leitrim: The Irish Revolution 1912–23' (PhD thesis, Dublin City University, 2018; publication forthcoming, Four Courts Press, 2019)

Muldoon, Rita, collection of letters, documents, photographs and diary or personal account, in the possession of her grandson, Kenneth Donnelly

Archives

Ardagh & Clonmacnois Diocesan Archives

Clongowes College Archives

Leitrim County Library, Local Studies Department

Military Archives

National Archives of Ireland

Plunkett, David, collection of IRA documents from the Maurice 'Moss' Twomey Archive

Royal College of Physicians of Ireland Archival Records

UCD Archives

Newspapers

Connacht Tribune

Irish Independent

Kerry News

Leitrim Observer

Longford Leader

Orlando Evening Star

The Cork Examiner

The Freeman's Journal

The Leitrim Advertiser

The Irish Times

Weekly Irish Times

Websites
www.irishtimes.com
www.libertyellisfoundation.org
www.militaryarchives.ie
www.oireachtas.ie

Interviews
Joe Griffin
Padraig Leyden
David Logan
Thomas Melia

Other Sources
RTÉ *Documentary On One*, 'An Unholy Trinity', August 2017

ACKNOWLEDGEMENTS

We owe a deep debt of gratitude to the grandchildren of Paddy and Rita Muldoon, and their Ryan, Griffin and Faulkner relatives, for trusting us with Rita Muldoon's personal papers, as well as family memories, photographs and other documents. We were also heavily reliant on the exceptional Local Studies Department of Leitrim County Library, Ballinamore, for the Thomas William Muldoon interview and other related documents, and on the unfailing assistance of Fr Tom Murray for access to the archives of the Diocese of Ardagh and Clonmacnois. We would also like to thank the families of those other Leitrim casualties of the Civil War to whom we spoke, and the staff of the archival facilities and other libraries to which we referred.

Special thanks must go to the RTÉ radio *Documentary on One* team for their help in telling the story as the radio documentary 'An Unholy Trinity' in August 2017: Liam O'Brien, Nicoline Greer, Sarah Blake, Ronan Kelly, Donal O'Herlihy and Richard McCullough. A special mention to Denis Reynolds for setting us on our way, and to the following for contributions to the documentary and book: Dawn Bradfield, Joe Taylor, Alan Torney, Brian Leyden, Stephen Faul, Prin Duignan, Jennifer Redmond, John Reynolds, David Plunkett, Cormac Ó Súilleabháin, Pádraig

Óg Ó Ruairc, Pat McGarty, Thomas Melia, Padraig Leyden, Brian Reade, Fiona Slevin, Harriet Wheelock, Deanne Ortiz, Thomas Kelly, Pat Curran, Eamon Courtney, David Logan, Orla and Raymond Palmer, Bernard Reynolds, Tom Boyle, Arthur Boyle, Katie Boyle, Kevin Terry, Simon Hugh-Jones and Mark Ruddy.

Tim would also like to thank his daughters, Aoife Kelly-Desmond and Etain O'Keeffe, for their encouragement and advice, and his wife, Adrienne, for everything else. Ken would like to thank his daughters, Alison King and Shauna Boyle, and his son, Robert Boyle, for their encouragement, and also their mother, Paula King, for her very generous technical support. He would also like to thank his sister, Deirdre Terry, and his brothers, Grell, Ronan, Kealan and Damien Boyle, for their help and encouragement.